simple
chocolate
step-by-step

Thunder Bay
P·R·E·S·S

San Diego, California

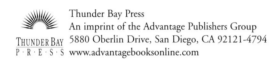

Thunder Bay Press
An imprint of the Advantage Publishers Group
5880 Oberlin Drive, San Diego, CA 92121-4794
www.advantagebooksonline.com

All notations of errors or omissions should be addressed to Thunder Bay Press, editorial department, at the above address. All other correspondence (author inquiries, permissions) concerning the content of this book should be addressed to The Foundry at the below address.

The Foundry
8035 Enterprise Street
Burnaby, BC V5A 1V7, U.K.
Tel: 44 604 415-2444 Fax: 44 604 415-3444
email: main@select-books.com

ISBN 1-57145-749-6

Library of Congress Cataloging-in-Publication Data available upon request.

Printed in Korea.

1 2 3 4 5   06 05 04 03 02

ACKNOWLEDGMENTS

Authors: Catherine Atkinson, Juliet Barker, Liz Martin, Carol Tennant, Mari Mererid Williams, and Elizabeth Wolf-Cohen
Editorial Consultant: Gina Steer
Project Editor: Karen Fitzpatrick
Photography: Colin Bowling and Paul Forrester
Home Economists and Stylists: Jacqueline Bellefontaine, Mandy Phipps, Vicki Smallwood, and Penny Stephens
Design Team: Helen Courtney, Jennifer Bishop, Lucy Bradbury, and Chris Herbert

All props supplied by Barbara Stewart at Surfaces

NOTE
Recipes using uncooked eggs should be avoided by infants,
the elderly, pregnant women, and anyone with a compromised immune system.

Special thanks to everyone involved in this book, particularly
Karen Fitzpatrick and Gina Steer.

CONTENTS

COOKIES

BARS & MUFFINS

DESSERTS

TARTS & PIES

DESSERTS

CAKES

Chocolate Around the World

The taste, texture, and versatility of chocolate has made it a favorite dessert and cooking ingredient throughout the world. In many countries, particularly in the western world, chocolate is closely associated with special celebrations and romantic occasions. Every country has its favorite flavorings: British chocolate often has added vanilla, Italy and France enjoy nut-based chocolate, especially hazelnuts and almonds, and the French like unsweetened chocolate. Most chocolate sold in the U.S. is semisweet chocolate, whereas Spanish chocolate is richly spiced.

GREAT BRITAIN

In Britain more money is spent on chocolate than on any of the basic essentials, such as bread or milk. Statistics show that more than a staggering $5 billion is spent on chocolate each year; 15 lbs. of chocolate is eaten by the average Briton annually, and the highest concentration of sales is at Easter, when over 16,000 tons of chocolate eggs are consumed.

Generally, British chocolate is sweeter than continental varieties and is made with caramelized milk crumb. It can also contain up to five percent vegetable fat, which lowers cost. Some European makers, however, insist that "real" chocolate must contain a hundred percent cocoa fat. Even so, Britain still has the second highest consumption of chocolate in the world! The Swiss had the monopoly on

semisweet chocolate until Cadbury produced Dairy Milk in 1905; it was an instant success. Cadbury's Milk Tray, which was made a few years later, is still one of the most popular boxes of chocolate, and Kit Kat, a chocolate-covered wafer first made in 1937, continues to be one of the best-sellers today.

In the last few years, there has been an increasing demand for more "sophisticated" chocolates with a higher percentage of cocoa solids. Charbonnel et Walker, despite its French-sounding name, was one of Britain's earliest producers of chocolates. Madame Charbonnel from the Maison Boissier chocolate house in Paris teamed up with Mrs. Walker to produce a huge range of elegant and lavish chocolate truffles.

Ackermans is a small family firm, founded around fifty years ago, and is now one of the major producers of handmade chocolates in Britain. Bendicks of Mayfair was started in the 1920s by Colonel Benson and Mr. Dickson, and is famed for peppermint chocolates (a very British taste that is not shared by other countries). Violet and rose fondant creams are another almost exclusively British taste.

UNITED STATES

In the U.S., consumers share the British liking for sweet chocolate and the market is dominated by a small number of mass-producers. Milton Hershey, a cocoa manufacturer, was so fascinated by the German chocolate manufacturing machinery he saw at the Chicago Exposition in the 1830s that he bought the exhibit. In 1903 he built his first chocolate factory, and today the Hershey bar is the most popular U.S. chocolate; it is slightly darker but even sweeter than most British chocolate. It was used as part of the emergency rations for the U.S. forces in the Second

World War and the town of Hershey in Pennsylvania has become a chocolate theme park.

Chocolate chips were created especially for inclusion in the Toll House chocolate chip cookie and are now sold in many countries.

SWITZERLAND

The Swiss boast the highest consumption of chocolate in the world. Switzerland's renowned semisweet chocolate is very delicate and smooth, due to Lindt's inventions of the conching machine, which blends chocolate to a silky texture. In most countries, manufacturers make their chocolate with powdered milk, but the Nestlé factory at Broc uses only fresh milk for its Cailler chocolate.

Suchard is another long-established company that makes the semisweet chocolate bar Milka and now produces Toblerone bars (although these were originally made by the innovator Jean Tobler). The triangular shape of the Toblerone bar represents the Swiss Alps, and it is made with a blend of chocolate, nougat, and almonds.

FRANCE

The French chocolate industry is made up of many small, independent firms who carefully guard their secret recipes. On the whole, unsweetened, strongly flavored chocolate is preferred.

ITALY

Italians enjoy sweet chocolate, frequently flavored with nuts, especially chestnuts, almonds, and hazelnuts. Large bars of chocolate are rarely sold; most chocolate comes wrapped and in bite-size pieces, such as the famous Neapolitans, which resemble individual chocolate bars and are sold throughout Europe.

BELGIUM

Belgium is renowned worldwide for its chocolate truffles and chocolate-covered pralines. Godiva chocolates were created in 1929 by the Drap family, who recognized that there was a demand for luxury chocolates following the austere war years. The chocolates are now exported worldwide.

AUSTRIA

Austria is as famous for its chocolate patisserie as its confectionery. Sachertorte is perhaps one of the best known chocolate cakes; it is a very rich, dense chocolate cake with an apricot glaze and a smooth, dark, glossy chocolate frosting.

GERMANY

German manufacturers produce high quality chocolates, similar to those enjoyed by the Swiss—the Germans are the third largest consumers of chocolate in Europe. The chocolates are often made with fresh ingredients.

THE NETHERLANDS

The Dutchman Conrad van Houten revolutionized the chocolate industry with his cocoa press in 1878. Today, the industry concentrates on making cocoa rather than chocolates. Unsweetened cocoa is exported from the Netherlands throughout the world.

SPAIN

The Spanish produce wonderful chocolates made with combinations of Mediterranean fruits and nuts, including bittersweet Seville oranges, almonds, and pine nuts. They also enjoy chocolate milk and hot chocolate, which is sold in a powdered form. More often, however, a solid bar of chocolate is broken into pieces and dissolved in cups of frothy, hot milk.

MEXICO

When the Spanish conquerors first arrived in Mexico in 1492, they found a wealth of new ingredients. One of their greatest discoveries was chocolate—the Aztecs made a drink from the beans of the cacao tree, and this idea was taken back to Spain and quickly spread to the rest of Europe. It is therefore surprising that in Mexico, chocolate as a dessert has never really caught on; the main use for chocolate is still as a beverage. Mexicans are fond of a chocolate corn drink known as *champurrada* and the classic frothy Mexican hot chocolate. These are often served at breakfast time with *churros*—deep-fried pastry fritters or with *pan dulce,* a sweet bread.

Mexican chocolate is made using unsweetened bitter cacao, which is blended with sugar, ground almonds, and cinnamon and pressed into round disks. The chocolate is grainy and crumbly when broken and is sold in packages, each containing five or six individually wrapped disks.

IN LOVE WITH CHOCOLATE

What makes chocolate so alluring? The Aztecs believed that chocolate had special powers, so it was served as a wedding-feast drink and to their emperor Montezuma before he retired to his harem. Cassanova confessed to a cup or two before wooing his lovers, and Madame du Barry made the excuse of keeping chocolate truffles "for tempting male consorts." Did they know that chocolate contains alkaloids, organic substances found in plants that can stimulate the brain and keep us alert? One of these is phenylethylamine, an endorphin that produces a high, similar to the feeling of being in love. Small amounts of caffeine and theobromine are also found in chocolate, and these stimulants may give chocolate its rumored aphrodisiac effects. Despite these scientific explanations, however, it could be that we love chocolate for much simpler reasons; it has to be one of the most luxurious and tempting foods ever known.

Although high in calories, chocolate also contains many nutrients, including protein, iron, calcium, magnesium, potassium, vitamin A, and the B vitamins. It certainly gives a quick energy boost and is often carried by mountaineers and astronauts, and has been included in soldiers' rations in the last two world wars.

The Origin of Chocolate

Chocolate, made from the cacao bean, originally came from the New World and was introduced to the Old World by Hernando Cortés (1485–1547) in the sixteenth century. It is now eaten extensively by both young and old alike. It is used to flavor drinks, candies, and ice cream, and is the foundation of many rich and luscious desserts. Today, France, Peru, and Bolivia are the only countries that prepare chocolate drinks from blocks of chocolate; in most other countries, cocoa (or cacao) powder is normally used.

A certain amount of confusion exists concerning the derivation of the word "chocolate." Some believe that it derives from the Aztec word *xocoatl*, meaning "bitter water." Others think that it originates from the Mexican word *atle*, meaning "water," and some believe that that the word is *onomatopoeic*, as the word "choco" represents the noise that water makes when it is stirred into a cup. The derivation of the word "cocoa" is simple, however, as it is from the Mexican word *cacao*, and in many countries, this is the word that is used. It is only in English that the word "cocoa" is used; it is thought that the British could not pronounce the word *cacao*. Whatever its origins, there can be no doubt that chocolate in all its forms has to be one of the most popular of all foods; there are many people who are confirmed chocoholics and could not imagine life without it.

THE HISTORY OF CHOCOLATE

The Aztecs and Mayans drank frothy *chocolatl*—a drink made from roasted and ground cacao beans mixed with various types of chili peppers and other spices—which was served cold. It had a bitter and pungent flavor, and was consumed at all special occasions, whether to celebrate a birth, a marriage, or as an offering to the gods. For this reason, it was often referred to as "food for the gods." It was also given as a reward to the valiant and strong men who fought to protect the villages from invasion. As well as being used to make *chocolatl*, cacao beans were used as currency throughout Central America to buy slaves, women, and even food.

Although Christopher Columbus (*c.* 1451–1506) certainly brought the cacao bean back to Europe, it did not become popular until Cortés introduced it to the Spanish king, Charles V, with whom this new drink was a favorite. It very slowly spread across Europe during the next two centuries, and finally became popular in the seventeenth century, resulting in the opening of fashionable chocolate houses.

The Spanish changed the drink, which was pungent and bitter, by adding vanilla and sugar to make it sweet (vanilla and sugar were two other new foods that were imported from the New World at the time). The ingredients of this new drink were a closely guarded secret, and a cup of this exotic beverage was extremely expensive, so only the wealthy could afford to drink it in the chocolate houses.

It was the English who began to add milk to the drink, but the high cost of importing the bean to England kept it from becoming popular, until William Ewart Gladstone (1809–1898),

who was Chancellor of the Exchequer at the time, lowered the import tax. The drink became fashionable in London and then slowly spread to the rest of Britain. From then on, chocolate grew in popularity, so much that today there are very few people in the world who are not aware of its properties. It is reputed by many to be an aphrodisiac and contains two stimulants, caffeine and theobromine, which explains the

feelings of well-being and the "high" experienced after eating chocolate.

TYPES OF CHOCOLATE

When using chocolate for cooking, as with all other foods, it is best to use the highest-quality chocolate that you can afford. Check the label for the cocoa butter content; this will enable you to ascertain the quality of the chocolate. Avoid chocolate substitutes, as these are far inferior to real chocolate and do not give as good a result.

Couverture Obtainable in both milk and plain varieties; it is the best chocolate available and has a high cocoa butter content. It can be found in specialty stores and is also available by mail order.

Bittersweet A good-quality chocolate with a high percentage of cocoa butter, normally around 72 percent; it is more readily available than couverture.

Unsweetened This can be difficult to find. If unobtainable, substitute 3 tablespoons of cocoa powder and 1 tablespoon of butter. If using in place of sweetened chocolate, adjust the sweetness of the recipe.

Plain (dark) This is the most popular; it has a reasonable cocoa butter content and is suitable for both cooking and eating.

Milk chocolate Sweeter than plain, it does not give a good result, as the cocoa butter content is lower, making the flavor and richness of the finished dish less satisfying.

White chocolate Does not contain any cocoa solids, but has cocoa butter; some types of white chocolate contain vegetable oil as well. It is normally used for decorating, rather than for baking, although it can be used in baking, if desired.

MANUFACTURE

Cocoa, and therefore chocolate, comes from small trees that are grown in many parts of Africa and the Americas. In Africa, the trees are often found on small farms of between 2–5 acres, whereas in the Americas, the farms are much larger, often operating through a cooperative system or as a large business enterprise.

The cocoa tree, *Theobroma cacao,* can grow to 30–40 ft., but in order to aid harvesting, the trees are pruned to ensure that they do not exceed 15–20 ft.

in height. There is little cultivation required apart from clearing the undergrowth. After planting, the seedlings grow rapidly and begin to bloom. They bear fruit after three to four years, and reach their full potential after eight years; the trees often last for thirty to forty years. However, to combat disease and increase or maintain productivity, it is recommended that the trees be replaced after twenty years.

A mature tree can produce, on average, 6,000 small pink flowers that grow on the trunk and main branches; about twenty of these flowers will mature into a cacao bean pod. The pods range in color from yellow-orange to

dark red and purple, and will ripen at different times of the year, although most of the harvesting is done between September and March. The pods are cut from the trees using a goulette, which is a long stick with a sharpened knife at the end, similar in appearance to a machete. The tough, fibrous outer casing of the pod is opened and about 25–30 seeds are scooped out with the pulp, then allowed to ferment.

The fermentation takes place under a high temperature and lasts between three to twelve days. The liquid that is extracted from the pulp, called "sweatings," is drained away, then the residue is stirred and mixed to ensure an even fermentation. The process reaches a temperature of 115°F, which kills the germs in the seeds and also changes the flavor and character of the

bean. The heat plumps the bean, filling it with moisture, and the inside becomes reddish-brown in color, with the heavy, heady flavor and aroma of cocoa. The pulp is then removed and the beans are dried, either by the sun or artificially. When the water content has decreased to eight percent, they are packaged and are ready for shipping. A mature tree will produce between 1–2 lbs. of "cured" cacao bean.

American cacao bean growers process the beans themselves, and over forty percent of the total amount produced is consumed in the United States. Canada, Australia, India, and some European countries, including France, Switzerland, and England, also process the beans. After shipping and arrival at their destination, the beans are washed, then roasted to develop their aroma and flavor. This roasting also aids the production process, making them easier to crack open, which is often done by a rolling process. After cracking the pieces, known as "nibs," they are "winnowed" to remove the fibrous shells. These shells are sometimes used to make cocoa tea, but are normally used in cattle feed.

The nibs are then graded and blended to produce the flavors required and are ground to a paste, often through stone mills. During this grinding, cocoa butter and a liquid known as "chocolate liquor" are extracted, which on cooling sets into a hard block. Half or more of this block is cocoa butter and is a pure fat. From this, the various types of chocolate are formed.

Equipment

Chocolate has a reputation for being difficult to work with, but a few pieces of well-chosen equipment make the job much easier. Although you can get by with just a selection of basic items, the following list provides a more comprehensive set of equipment for the serious chocolatier.

Bowls A selection of bowls in a variety of sizes in glass, metal, or ceramic are all suitable for working with chocolate, as these materials distribute the heat well and are suitable for use on the burner, over hot water, and in the microwave. Plastic is less versatile as it can only be used in the microwave.

Candy thermometer This is very useful, especially if tempering chocolate (see Handling chocolate, p.14).

Chocolate forks These are very fine forks, similar to fondue forks but with longer prongs. Sometimes the points of the prongs are joined and curved. They are very useful for coating truffles and handling chocolate-dipped items. They are also very expensive, however, and are really only for the dedicated chocolate maker.

Cooling rack If items are left to cool in pans or on cookie sheets, they are likely to create steam as they cool, which will be trapped by the pan or cookie sheet.

Cookies will not be crisp, and cakes may become soggy.

Decorating bag with fine tip This is a small nylon decorating bag with a variety of tips that is very useful for decorating cakes and, when fitted with a plain tip, for drizzling chocolate.

Dredger This is useful both for confectioners' sugar and unsweetened cocoa and is less messy than using a strainer. Dredgers are also good for dusting finished chocolates or cakes.

Fine-mesh cooling rack This is great for setting dipped items. Put the rack over a plate to catch drips and put coated items on it to set. Larger, meshed cake cooling racks are not suitable but can be adapted by being covered with nonstick baking parchment.

Grater The coarser side of a box grater is useful for making decorations.

Kitchen forks/skewers These are an affordable alternative to specialty chocolate forks. Kitchen forks and skewers can be used to handle dipped items. Using skewers, items can be speared before being dipped (fruit or truffles). Harder items such as cookies should be dipped using two forks. Both items are more likely to leave marks on the chocolate than specialty forks.

Large sharp knife Good for cutting shapes out of a set sheet of chocolate or for making chocolate caraque.

Marble slab This is also useful in pastry making as it stays cool regardless of the kitchen temperature. Melted chocolate can be poured directly onto the marble, either in a sheet for making curls or caraque, or for making shapes.

Metal spatulas These are long thin blades with rounded ends, though they come in different sizes. The blades are flexible and are very useful for spreading melted chocolate, either onto cakes or cookies or onto marble slabs for making chocolate decorations.

Microwave oven This is good for melting chocolate. Most packages of chocolate will have instructions for melting using a microwave, but you will need to know the power of your oven. This is usually indicated on the door panel or on the control panel and will either be a letter rating or a number indicating wattage. It is important not to overheat the chocolate, so the best method is to use the microwave in bursts of 30 seconds, stirring well between bursts.

Molds A large variety of molds for making chocolates is available from

specialty stores and by mail order. Sometimes made of rigid material, flexible plastic molds are the easiest to use. There are three methods for using the molds, depending on the desired result. Method one, best for making small chocolate shapes, is to pour melted chocolate into the mold and leave until set. Method two, for making large, hollow shapes, like Easter eggs, is to pour chocolate into the mold until about one-third full, then tilt the mold until the inside is completely coated with a layer of chocolate, then pour off any excess. Method three is to use a paintbrush dipped in melted chocolate to paint the inside of the mold with a thin layer. Repeat the process using thin layers until the chocolate is set firm. This is the best method to use if your mold is unconventional, a baking cup, for example. The plastic molds can then simply be bent and flexed until the chocolate comes loose. These produce excellent results and the chocolate emerges from the mold with a beautiful shiny surface. If using a baking cup, remove carefully, possibly in strips.

Paint scraper A clean paint scraper is the best tool for making chocolate curls. It is well worth purchasing one and keeping it for this purpose.

Pastry cutters These are mainly useful for cutting shapes out of chocolate that has set in a sheet. These can then be used for sandwiching a filling or for decorating cakes.

Petit four cases These cases are available in large supermarkets and kitchenware stores. They come in a variety of sizes and colors, and are perfect for displaying handmade chocolates, especially if they are being packaged in a box.

Petit four cutters As with pastry cutters, these are very useful for making small shapes for use as decorations.

Rubber spatulas These are available in small, medium, and large sizes, including one that is spoon shaped.

Saucepans All kitchens will have a set of saucepans, but for chocolate cooking

they need to be fairly small so that a heatproof bowl can sit snugly on top without touching the bottom of the saucepan. Alternatively, glass double boilers are also very useful. The top saucepan sits in the bottom one, with a large gap for water between them. They were originally designed for making sauces such as Hollandaise, which do not require the bottom of the saucepan to get any direct heat and so are perfect for melting all types of chocolate.

Small paintbrush/pastry brush Brushes are most useful for making molded chocolates in unusual shapes but are also good for painting the inside of pastry shells with chocolate before filling with fruit or cream.

Strainer This is useful for sifting unsweetened cocoa and confectioners' sugar, both of which are a bit sticky and may have lumps that need removing.

Vegetable peeler This is excellent for making chocolate curls quickly from a bar of chocolate. They will be smaller and coarser than curls made using set chocolate but can be an effective decoration on top of a cake.

Waxed/baking parchment These are both essential for lining cake pans. Also available are reusable nonstick mats, which can be cut to size and used again and again. Nonstick baking parchment is good for making small, disposable decorating bags that are perfect for drizzling chocolate or frosting onto cakes and cookies. Take a piece of waxed paper, about 8 inches square, and fold it in half diagonally to make a double triangle. Fold the paper around to form a cone, making the point at the center of the long edge. Tighten the cone until all the points meet, then fold the points of paper down into the top of the cone. You can now fill the cone and then carefully snip off the bottom to make a decorating bag.

Types of Chocolate

Unsweetened cooking chocolate is the type used in baking. It comes in varying degrees of bitterness, depending on the percentage of cocoa solids it contains. Unsweetened cooking chocolate usually contains at least seventy percent cocoa solids. This is the darkest and bitterest chocolate, and has the least amount of added sugar. Next is bittersweet cooking chocolate, which is semisweet and should contain at least fifty percent cocoa solids. This is probably the most versatile unsweetened chocolate. Finally, unsweetened eating chocolate, which may contain as little as twenty-five percent cocoa solids, is the sweetest and least suitable for cooking. The price of the chocolate is a good indication of its quality. Specialist chocolate sellers will also be able to tell you the variety of cacao. Most commercial chocolate is produced from Forastero, but the finest chocolates are made using beans from the Criollo or Trinitario varieties.

Semisweet chocolate, invented in 1879 by Swiss manufacturer Daniel Peter, contains milk powder and a higher percentage of sugar than unsweetened chocolate. The percentage of cocoa solids in semisweet chocolate is generally quite low, but good-quality brands are available containing as much as forty percent. Semisweet chocolate is smoother and stickier in the mouth than unsweetened chocolate and is always much sweeter, making it a favorite with children. Semisweet chocolate is not suitable for cooking as it is difficult to set, being sensitive to temperature, but is useful for decoration.

White chocolate is not chocolate, as it contains no cocoa solids. It is made with cocoa butter only, along with milk solids and sugar. Better-quality brands use a higher proportion of cocoa butter while cheaper brands use vegetable oils and artificial flavorings. White chocolate is very sweet and sensitive to heat but combines well with many other flavors, particularly fruit.

Couverture is the chocolate most commonly used by professional chocolatiers. It has a high cocoa butter content and no added fats, which means that it melts smoothly and thinly. This makes it easier to handle, and it is especially good for coating chocolates and truffles. Couverture will usually be tempered before use (see Handling Chocolate, p. 14). It is expensive and is available from specialty suppliers or by mail order. It is available in unsweetened, semisweet, and white varieties.

Chocolate cake covering often contains very little chocolate but is more often flavored with cocoa powder. It has a waxy texture but is easy to use as it spreads and sets easily.

Cocoa powder is made by reducing the cocoa butter content of the cacao nib by pressing it through a hydraulic press. This produces a cake, which can then be pulverized into a fine powder. Alkaline salts are then added to keep the powder from caking and to make it more easy to mix. This is known as "Dutching," because it was invented by Dutch chocolate maker Conrad J. van Houten.

Hot chocolate is a mixture of unsweetened cocoa, sugar, and sometimes milk powder. It is mixed into hot milk or water to make a drink. There are also chocolate mixes that are added to cold milk, and these are popular with children.

SUGARS AND CHOCOLATE FLAVORINGS

In baking, darker, unrefined sugars are often used with chocolate to add depth of flavor. Brown sugar and dark brown sugar are particularly well suited to chocolate. However, if purity of flavor is what is needed, granulated sugar is probably the best option; vanilla sugar is also a good choice.

Coffee is a classic flavor to accompany chocolate. Mixed together, the flavor is known as "mocha." Coffee adds a wonderful flavor to chocolate cakes, cookies, and drinks.

Vanilla is the perfect foil for chocolate and seems to enhance rather than mask it. Many chocolate brands add vanilla to their chocolate during the manufacturing process.

A number of other spices also combine well with chocolate, including cinnamon, star anise, nutmeg, and cloves. Cardamom goes particularly well with white chocolate.

Caramel is also very good with chocolate. Try a chocolate-flavored crème brûlée, for example, or decorate chocolate cakes with caramel shapes.

The citrus flavors of orange and lemon cut through the creamy richness of chocolate. Candied orange slices are often dipped in very fine unsweetened chocolate—these are ideal with coffee or for decorating cakes.

Summer fruits go very well with chocolate. Strawberries are often dipped in chocolate, which is then left to set, but chocolate and raspberries are an often overlooked yet delicious combination. White chocolate in particular combines well with berries, especially if a little lemon is added.

Orchard fruits have less affinity with chocolate, but pears are the exception. Pears poached in vanilla syrup, then baked in a chocolate and almond frangipane or served with chocolate sauce are two classic desserts.

Chocolate and alcohol are a very successful combination, particularly in truffles and desserts. Try rum, brandy, whiskey, and fruit-flavored liqueurs, such as Cointreau, framboise, and cassis.

Toasted nuts make an excellent addition to chocolate cookies, cakes, and desserts. Almonds, hazelnuts, pecans, walnuts, macadamias, and Brazil nuts all work well with chocolate.

Mint, which is available fresh, dried, and as an extract, makes an excellent partner to chocolate.

Dried fruit mixes well with chocolate. Try raisins, golden raisins, currants, apricots, figs, and dried cherries. Dried fruit also mixes together with nuts.

Cream and chocolate are a classic combination used to best effect when making ganache or truffles. Cream is heated to the boiling point and then poured over chopped or grated chocolate. This is then stirred until smooth. Once cool and starting to set, ganache can be used for making truffles or for covering and filling cakes.

Handling Chocolate:
Tips & Techniques

There are a few useful techniques for working with chocolate. None of them are very complicated, and all can be mastered easily with a little practice.

These general guidelines apply equally for all types of chocolate.

MELTING CHOCOLATE

All types of chocolate are sensitive to temperature, so care needs to be taken during the melting process. It is also worth noting that different brands of chocolate have different consistencies when melting and when melted. Experiment with different brands to find one that you prefer.

As a general rule, it is important not to allow any water to come into contact with the chocolate. In fact, a drop or two of water is more dangerous than larger amounts, which may blend in. The melted chocolate will seize and it will be impossible to bring it back to a smooth consistency.

Do not overheat chocolate or melt it by itself in a pan over a direct heat. Always use either a double boiler or a heatproof bowl set over a saucepan of water, but do not allow the bottom of the bowl to come into contact with the water, as this would overheat the chocolate. Keep an eye on the chocolate, checking it every couple of minutes and reducing or extinguishing the heat under the saucepan, as necessary. Stir the chocolate once or twice during

melting until it is smooth and no lumps remain. Do not cover the bowl once the chocolate has melted, or condensation will form, water will drop into it, and it will be ruined. If the chocolate turns from a glossy, liquid mass into a dull, coarse, textured mess, you will have to start over.

Microwaving is another way of melting chocolate but again, caution is required. Follow the oven manufacturer's instructions together with the instructions on the chocolate and proceed with care. Melt the chocolate in bursts of 30–60 seconds, stirring well between bursts until the chocolate is smooth. If possible, stop microwaving before all the chocolate has melted and allow the residual heat in the chocolate to finish the job. The advantage of microwaving is that you do not need to use a saucepan, making the whole job quicker and neater.

MAKING CHOCOLATE DECORATIONS

Curls and caraque Chocolate curls are made using a clean paint scraper. They are usually large, fully formed curls which are useful for decorating cakes. Caraque are long thin curls, which can be used in the same way.

To make either shape, melt the chocolate following your preferred method and then spread it in a thin layer over a cool surface, such as a marble slab, ceramic tile or a piece of

granite. Leave until just set but not hard.

To make curls, take the clean paint scraper and set it at an angle to the surface of the chocolate, then push, taking a layer off the surface. This will curl until you release the pressure.

To make caraque, use a large sharp knife and hold it at about a 45-degree angle to the chocolate. Hold the handle and the tip, and scrape the knife toward you, pulling the handle but keeping the tip more or less in the same place. This method makes thinner, tighter, longer curls.

Shaved chocolate Using a vegetable peeler, shave a thick block of chocolate to make minicurls. These are best achieved if the chocolate is a little soft, otherwise it has a tendency to break into little flakes.

Chocolate shapes Spread a thin layer of chocolate, as described in the instructions for chocolate curls, and allow to set as before. Use shaped cutters or a sharp knife to cut out shapes. Use to decorate cakes.

Chocolate leaves Many types of leaves are suitable, but ensure they are not poisonous before using. Rose leaves are easy to find and make good shapes. Wash and dry the leaves carefully before using. Melt chocolate following the instructions given at the beginning of the section. Using a small paintbrush, paint a thin layer of chocolate onto the back of the leaf. Allow to set before adding another thin layer. When set, carefully peel off the leaf. Chocolate leaves are also very attractive when made using two different types of chocolate, white and unsweetened chocolate, for example. Paint half the leaf first with one type of chocolate and allow to set before painting the other half with the second chocolate. Allow to set, then peel off the leaf as above.

Chocolate lace Make a piping bag out of nonstick baking parchment (see Equipment, p.11). Draw an outline of the required shape onto some nonstick baking parchment, a triangle, for example. Pipe chocolate evenly onto the outline, fill in the center with lacy squiggles, and leave until set. Remove the paper to use.

Chocolate squiggles Use a teaspoon of melted chocolate to drizzle random shapes onto nonstick parchment paper. Allow to set, and remove the paper to use. Alternatively, pipe a zigzag line about 2 inches long onto a piece of nonstick baking parchment. Pipe a straight line slightly longer at either end down the center of the zigzag.

Chocolate butterflies Draw a butterfly shape on a piece of nonstick parchment paper. Fold the paper down the center of the body of the butterfly to make a crease, then open the paper out flat. Pipe chocolate onto the outline of the butterfly, then fill in the wings with loose zigzag lines. Carefully fold the

paper so the wings are at right angles, supporting them from underneath in the corner of a large pan or with some other support, and leave until set. Peel away the paper to use.

Chocolate modeling paste To make chocolate modeling paste (very useful for cake covering and for making heavier shapes like ribbons), put 7 squares unsweetened chocolate in a bowl and add 3 tablespoons of liquid glucose. Set the bowl over a saucepan of gently simmering water. Stir until the chocolate is just melted, then remove from the heat. Beat until smooth and let the mixture cool. When cool enough to handle, knead to a smooth paste on a clean surface. The mixture can be rolled and cut to shape. If the paste hardens, wrap it in plastic wrap and warm it in the microwave for a few seconds on low.

CARAMEL AND PRALINE DECORATIONS

Caramel Put ⅓ cup of granulated sugar into a heavy saucepan with about 3 tablespoons of cold water. Over a low heat, stir well until the sugar has dissolved completely. If any sugar clings to the saucepan, brush it down using a wet brush. Bring the mixture to a boil and cook, without stirring, until the mixture turns golden. You may need to tilt the saucepan carefully to ensure the sugar colors evenly. As soon as the desired color is reached, remove the saucepan from the heat and plunge the bottom of the saucepan into cold water to keep it from cooking further.

Praline To make pralines, follow the instructions as for caramel, but during the final stage do not plunge the saucepan into cold water. Add nuts to the caramel mixture. Do not stir, but pour immediately onto a greased cookie sheet. Allow to set at room temperature. Once cold, the pralines can be chopped or broken into pieces as required. Keep leftover pralines in a sealed container. It will keep for several months if stored this way.

Caramel-dipped nuts To make the caramel, remove the saucepan from the heat, and plunge into cold water. Using two skewers, dip individual nuts into the hot caramel, lift out carefully, allowing excess to run off, then transfer to a foil-covered tray until set. If the caramel becomes too sticky or starts making a lot of sugar strands, reheat gently until liquid again.

Caramel shapes Make the caramel, remove the saucepan from the heat, and plunge into cold water as described earlier. Using a teaspoon, pour spoonfuls of caramel onto a greased cookie sheet. Allow to set before removing from the tray. Do not refrigerate caramel shapes, as they will liquefy.

Caramel lace Follow the method for caramel shapes, but use a teaspoon to drizzle threads in a random pattern onto a greased tray. When set, break into pieces. Do not refrigerate.

Chocolate Chip Cookies

1 Preheat the oven to 350° F. Lightly butter 3–4 large cookie sheets with 1 tablespoon of the butter. Place the remaining butter and both sugars in a food processor, and blend until smooth. Add the egg and vanilla extract, and blend briefly. Alternatively, cream the butter and sugars together in a large bowl, then beat in the egg with the vanilla extract.

2 If using a food processor, scrape out the batter with a spatula, and place the batter into a large bowl. Sift the flour and baking soda together, then fold into the creamed batter. When the batter is blended thoroughly, stir in the chocolate chips.

3 Drop heaping teaspoons of the batter onto the prepared cookie sheets. Make sure they are spaced well apart, as they will spread during cooking. Bake in the preheated oven for 10–12 minutes or until lightly golden.

4 Let cool for a few seconds, then using a spatula, transfer to a wire rack and cool completely. The cookies are best eaten when just cooked but can be stored in an airtight plastic container for a few days.

INGREDIENTS
Makes about 30

1 stick, plus 1 tbsp. butter
¼ cup sugar
⅓ cup firmly packed dark brown sugar
1 medium egg, beaten
½ tsp. vanilla extract
1 cup all-purpose flour
½ tsp. baking soda
¾ cup semisweet chocolate chips

Helpful Hint

For lightly textured, crumbly cookies, do not overwork the cookie dough. Handle as little as possible and fold the ingredients together gently using a metal spoon or rubber spatula. For a change, use an equal mixture of chocolate chips and nuts. Alternatively, replace the chocolate chips entirely with an equal quantity of your favorite chopped nuts.

Chewy Chocolate & Nut Cookies

1 Preheat the oven to 350° F. Lightly butter several cookie sheets with the butter, and line with a sheet of nonstick baking parchment. Place the egg whites in a large grease-free bowl, and beat with an electric mixer until the egg whites are very frothy.

2 Add the sugar, unsweetened cocoa, flour, and coffee powder, and beat again until the ingredients are blended thoroughly. Add 1 tablespoon of water, and beat on the highest speed until the mixture is very thick. Fold in the walnuts.

3 Place tablespoons of the batter onto the prepared cookie sheets, leaving plenty of space between them, as they expand greatly during cooking.

4 Bake in the preheated oven for 12–15 minutes or until the tops are firm, golden, and quite cracked. Let cool for 30 seconds, then transfer to a wire rack and let cool. Store in an airtight container.

INGREDIENTS
Makes 18

1 tbsp. butter
4 medium egg whites
3 cups confectioners' sugar
¾ cup unsweetened cocoa
2 tbsp. all-purpose flour
1 tsp. instant coffee powder
1 cup walnuts, finely chopped

Food Fact

When the Spanish brought the cocoa bean home, they also brought the word "cacao" as well. In European countries it is still known as cacao—it is only in the English language that it is known as cocoa.

Tasty Tip

Although the walnuts in these cookies are excellent, hazelnuts or mixed nuts would also go very well with both the chocolate and the coffee flavors.

White Chocolate Cookies

1 Preheat the oven to 350° F. Lightly butter several cookie sheets with 1 tablespoon of the butter. Place the remaining butter with both sugars into a large bowl and beat with a wooden spoon or an electric mixer until soft and fluffy.

2 Beat the egg, then gradually beat it into the creamed mixture. Sift the flour and the baking soda together, then carefully fold into the creamed mixture with a few drops of vanilla extract.

3 Coarsely chop the chocolate and hazelnuts into small pieces, add to the bowl, and gently stir into the batter. Mix together lightly to blend.

4 Spoon heaping teaspoons of the batter onto the prepared cookie sheets, making sure that there is plenty of space in between each one, as they will spread a lot during cooking.

5 Bake the cookies in the preheated oven for 10 minutes or until golden, then remove from the oven and let cool for 1 minute. Using a spatula, carefully transfer to a wire rack and let cool completely. The cookies are best eaten on the day they are made. Store in an airtight plastic container.

INGREDIENTS
Makes about 24

1 stick, plus 1 tbsp. butter
3 tbsp. sugar
⅓ cup firmly packed dark brown sugar
1 medium egg
1 cup all-purpose flour
½ tsp. baking soda
few drops of vanilla extract
5 squares white chocolate
½ cup whole hazelnuts, shelled

Helpful Hint

White chocolate is available in bars as well as in chips. As there are no cocoa solids in white chocolate, look for one with a good percentage of cocoa butter, as it is the cocoa butter that gives the chocolate its luscious, creamy texture.

Fudgy Chocolate Bars

INGREDIENTS
Makes 14

⅔ cup candied cherries

1 tbsp. shelled hazelnuts

5 squares unsweetened chocolate

1¼ sticks unsalted butter

¼ tsp. salt

1 cup graham crackers, chopped
  into ¼-in. pieces

1 tbsp. confectioners' sugar, sifted
  (optional)

1 Preheat the oven to 350° F. Lightly grease a 7-inch square pan, and line the base with nonstick baking parchment. Rinse the candied cherries thoroughly, dry well on paper towels, and set aside.

2 Place the nuts on a baking tray and roast in the preheated oven for 10 minutes or until light golden brown. Let cool slightly, then chop coarsely and set aside.

3 Break the chocolate into small pieces, and place with the butter and salt into the top of a double boiler or in a bowl set over a saucepan of gently simmering water. Heat gently, stirring until melted and smooth. Alternatively, melt the chocolate in the microwave according to the manufacturer's instructions.

4 Cut the cherries in half. Add to the chocolate mixture, along with the graham crackers and nuts, and stir well. Spoon the batter into the prepared pan and level the top.

5 Chill in the refrigerator for 30 minutes, remove from the pan, discard the baking parchment, and cut into 14 bars. Cover lightly, return to the refrigerator, and keep chilled until ready to serve. To serve, lightly sprinkle the bars with sifted confectioners' sugar, if desired. Cover with plastic wrap and store in the refrigerator.

Tasty Tip

For these bars, it is best to use unsweetened chocolate with around fifty percent cocoa solids. Bittersweet chocolate would not give a good flavor, as it is too bitter.

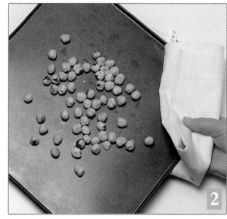

Chocolate Shortcake

1 Preheat the oven to 325° F. Lightly grease several cookie sheets and line with nonstick baking parchment. Place the butter, confectioners' sugar, and vanilla extract together in a food processor and blend briefly until smooth. Alternatively, using a wooden spoon, cream the butter, confectioners' sugar, and vanilla extract in a bowl.

2 Sift the flour, cocoa, and salt together, then either add to the food processor bowl and blend quickly to form a dough, or add to the bowl and, using your hands, mix together until a smooth dough is formed.

3 Turn the dough out onto a clean board lined with plastic wrap. Place another sheet of plastic wrap over the top and roll the dough out until it is ½ inch thick. Transfer the whole board to the refrigerator and chill for 1½–2 hours.

4 Remove the top piece of plastic wrap and use a 2-inch cutter to cut the dough into 30–32 rounds. Place the rounds on the prepared cookie sheets and bake in the preheated oven for about 15 minutes or until firm.

5 Cool for 1 minute, then using a spatula, carefully remove the shortcakes from the baking parchment and transfer to a wire rack. Let cool completely. Sprinkle the shortcakes with confectioners' sugar before serving. Store in an airtight plastic container for a few days.

INGREDIENTS
Makes 30–32

2 sticks unsalted butter, softened
1¼ cups confectioners' sugar
1 tsp. vanilla extract
2¼ cups all-purpose flour
¼ cup unsweetened cocoa
¼ tsp. salt
extra confectioners' sugar, sifted, to decorate

Food Fact

Using confectioners' sugar instead of granulated sugar helps to give these cookies a really crumbly texture. Make sure that you use butter rather than margarine to ensure that you get the classic shortbread texture.

Chocolate Macaroons

1 Preheat the oven to 350° F. Lightly grease several cookie sheets and line with sheets of nonstick baking parchment. Melt the chocolate in a heatproof bowl set over a saucepan of simmering water. Alternatively, melt in the microwave according to the manufacturer's instructions. Stir until smooth, then cool slightly.

2 Place the ground almonds in a food processor and add the sugar, almond extract, unsweetened cocoa, and one of the egg whites. Add the melted chocolate and a little of the other egg white, and blend to make a soft smooth paste. Alternatively, place the ground almonds with the sugar, almond extract, and cocoa in a bowl, and make a well in the center. Add the melted chocolate with sufficient egg white, and gradually blend together to form a smooth but not sticky paste.

3 Shape the dough into small balls the size of large walnuts, and place them on the prepared cookie sheets. Flatten them slightly, then brush with a little water. Sprinkle a little confectioners' sugar over them and cook in the preheated oven for 10–12 minutes or until just firm.

4 Using a spatula, carefully lift the macaroons off the baking parchment and transfer to a wire rack to cool. These are best served immediately but can be stored in an airtight container.

INGREDIENTS
Makes 20

2½ squares unsweetened chocolate
1 cup ground almonds
½ cup sugar
¼ tsp. almond extract
1 tbsp. unsweetened cocoa
2 medium egg whites
1 tbsp. confectioners' sugar

Helpful Hint

If you prefer, you could cook these cookies on edible rice paper, available from Asian grocers. Cover the baking tray with rice paper and drop the dough onto the paper as directed above. Bake in the preheated oven, then tear the paper to release the macaroons.

Chocolate & Ginger Florentines

1 Preheat the oven to 350° F. Lightly grease several baking trays. Melt the butter, cream, and sugar together in a saucepan, and bring slowly to a boil. Remove from the heat and stir in the almonds and the candied ginger.

2 Let cool slightly, then mix in the flour and the salt. Blend together, then place heaping teaspoons of the batter on the baking trays. Make sure they are spaced well apart, as they expand during cooking. Flatten them slightly with the back of a wet spoon.

3 Bake in the preheated oven for 10–12 minutes or until just brown at the edges. Let cool slightly. Using a spatula, carefully transfer the Florentines to a wire rack and let cool.

4 Melt the chocolate in a heatproof bowl set over a saucepan of gently simmering water. Alternatively, melt the chocolate in the microwave according to the manufacturer's instructions until just liquid and smooth. Spread thickly over one side of the Florentines, then mark wavy lines through the chocolate using a fork and leave until firm.

INGREDIENTS
Makes 14–16

3 tbsp. butter
5 tbsp. heavy cream
¼ cup sugar
½ cup chopped almonds
½ cup slivered almonds
1½ tbsp. candied ginger, chopped
¼ cup all-purpose flour
pinch of salt
5 squares unsweetened chocolate

Helpful Hint

These cookies spread quite a bit in the oven. To make evenly sized, nicely shaped cookies, try forming the cookies in a plain 3-inch pastry cutter as soon as they come out of the oven and are still very hot and pliable. When making these Florentines, only place 3–4 on each baking tray to ensure that they can be removed easily from the tray after cooking. Let cool for about 1 minute, then with a round-bladed knife, gently ease around the outside edge of each Florentine. Once they lift easily, transfer to a wire cooling rack.

Italian Biscotti

1 Preheat the oven to 375° F. Lightly grease 3–4 cookies sheets and set aside. Cream the butter and sugar together in a bowl, and mix in the vanilla extract. When it is light and fluffy, beat in the egg with the cinnamon, lemon rind, and the ground almonds. Stir in the flour to make a firm dough.

2 Knead lightly until smooth and free from cracks. Shape the dough into rectangular blocks about 1½ inches in diameter, wrap in waxed paper, and chill in the refrigerator for at least 2 hours.

3 Cut the chilled dough into ¼-inch slices, place on the cookie sheets, and cook in the preheated oven for 12–15 minutes or until firm. Remove from the oven, cool slightly, then transfer to wire racks to cool.

4 When completely cold, melt the chocolate in a heatproof bowl set over a saucepan of simmering water. Alternatively, melt the chocolate in the microwave according to the manufacturer's instructions. Spoon into a decorating bag and pipe over the cookies. Allow to dry on a sheet of nonstick baking parchment before serving.

INGREDIENTS
Makes 26–28

1¼ sticks butter
1 cup sugar
¼ tsp. vanilla extract
1 small egg, beaten
¼ tsp. ground cinnamon
1 tbsp. grated lemon rind
2 tbsp. ground almonds
1¼ cups all-purpose flour
5 squares unsweetened chocolate

Helpful Hint

When using vanilla extract, be sure to use extract and not vanilla flavoring, which is a cheap substitute. Alternatively, use vanilla sugar, which is very easy to make. Simply place a vanilla pod in a clean, airtight jar and fill with granulated sugar. Secure and leave in a cool, dark place for 2–3 weeks before using.

Food Fact

In Italy, these deliciously crunchy little cookies are traditionally served with a sweet dessert wine called *Vin Santo*.

Chocolate & Nut Refrigerator Cookies

1 Preheat the oven to 375° F. Lightly grease several large cookie sheets with 1 tablespoon of the butter. Cream the remaining butter and both sugars in a large bowl until light and fluffy, then gradually beat in the egg.

2 Sift the flour, baking soda, and unsweetened cocoa together, then gradually fold into the creamed batter together with the chopped pecans. Mix thoroughly until a smooth but stiff dough is formed.

3 Place the dough on a lightly floured surface and roll into sausage shapes about 2 inches in diameter. Wrap in plastic wrap and chill in the refrigerator for at least 12 hours or preferably overnight.

4 Cut the dough into thin slices and place on the prepared cookie sheets. Bake in the preheated oven for 8–10 minutes or until firm. Remove from the oven and let cool slightly. Using a spatula, transfer to a wire rack to cool. Store in an airtight plastic container.

INGREDIENTS
Makes 18

1½ sticks salted butter
⅔ cup firmly packed dark brown sugar
2 tbsp. granulated sugar
1 medium egg, beaten
1¾ cups all-purpose flour
½ tsp. baking soda
¼ cup unsweetened cocoa
1 cup pecans, finely chopped

Helpful Hint

This dough will keep in the refrigerator for four to five days if well wrapped. Cut off and bake a few cookies as needed. When greasing cookie sheets or baking trays for cookies, be careful about how much oil or butter you use, especially if using nonstick cookie sheets. Very rich mixtures that use a high proportion of fat will not need to be baked on greased cookie sheets. If they are, there is the probability that the cookies will spread too much.

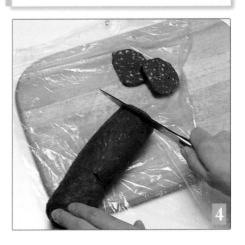

Chocolate & Hazelnut Cookies

1 Preheat the oven to 350° F. Lightly grease and flour 2–3 baking trays. Chop ¼ cup of the hazelnuts and set aside. Blend the remaining hazelnuts with the sugar in a food processor until finely ground. Add the butter to the processor bowl and then blend until pale and creamy.

2 Add the salt, unsweetened cocoa, and the heavy cream, and mix well. Scrape the batter into a bowl with a spatula, and stir in the egg whites. Sift the flour, then stir into the batter together with the rum.

3 Spoon heaping tablespoons of the batter onto the baking tray and sprinkle over a few of the remaining hazelnuts. Bake in the preheated oven for 5–7 minutes or until firm. Remove the cookies from the oven and let cool for 1–2 minutes. Using a spatula, transfer to wire racks and let cool.

4 When the cookies are cool, melt the chocolate in a heatproof bowl set over a saucepan of simmering water. Stir until smooth, then drizzle a little of the chocolate over the top of each cookie. Let dry on a wire rack before serving.

INGREDIENTS
Makes 12

¾ cup blanched hazelnuts
⅔ cup sugar
½ stick unsalted butter
pinch of salt
5 tsp. unsweetened cocoa
3 tbsp. heavy cream
2 large egg whites
2 tbsp. all-purpose flour
2 tbsp. rum
3 squares white chocolate

Helpful Hint

Be careful not to chop the hazelnuts for too long in the food processor, as this tends to make them very oily. To blanch hazelnuts or any nut, simply place on a baking tray and heat in a hot oven for 10 minutes. Remove, then place in a clean dishtowel and rub off the brown skins. Do not rub too many at a time, otherwise they may escape from the dishtowel.

Chocolate & Almond Cookies

1 Preheat the oven to 400° F. Lightly grease several cookie sheets. Cream the butter and confectioners' sugar together until light and fluffy, then gradually beat in the egg, beating well after each addition. When all the egg has been added, stir in the milk and lemon rind.

2 Sift the flour, then stir into the batter together with the chopped almonds to form a smooth and pliable dough. Wrap in plastic wrap and chill in the refrigerator for 2 hours.

3 Roll the dough out on a lightly floured surface, in a large oblong shape about ¼ inch thick. Cut into strips, about 2½ inches long and 1½ inches wide, and place on the prepared cookie sheets

4 Bake in the preheated oven for 15 minutes or until golden, then remove from the oven and let cool for a few minutes. Transfer to a wire rack and let cool completely.

5 Melt the chocolate in a small heatproof bowl set over a saucepan of simmering water. Alternatively, melt the chocolate in the microwave according to the manufacturer's instructions until smooth. Spread the chocolate thickly over the cookies, sprinkle over the toasted flaked or slivered almonds, and allow to set before serving.

INGREDIENTS
Makes 18–20

1 stick, plus 1 tbsp. butter
⅔ cup confectioners' sugar
1 medium egg, beaten
1 tbsp. milk
1 tbsp. grated lemon rind
2¼ cups all-purpose flour
1 cup blanched almonds, chopped
4 squares unsweetened chocolate
¾ cup flaked or slivered almonds, toasted

Tasty Tip

As an alternative to flaked almonds for decorating these cookies, use slivered almonds. They are easy to make; simply cut whole blanched almonds into thin slivers.

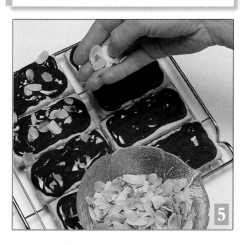

Fig & Chocolate Bars

1 Preheat the oven to 350° F. Lightly grease a 7-inch square cake pan. Place the butter and the flour in a large bowl and, using your fingertips, rub the butter into the flour until it resembles fine bread crumbs.

2 Stir in the sugar, then using your hand, bring the batter together to form a smooth dough. Knead until smooth, then press the dough into the prepared pan. Lightly prick the bottom with a fork and bake in the preheated oven for 20–30 minutes or until golden. Remove from the oven and let the shortbread cool in the pan until completely cooled.

3 Meanwhile, place the dried figs, lemon juice, ½ cup water, and the ground cinnamon in a saucepan, and bring to a boil. Cover and simmer for 20 minutes or until soft, stirring occasionally during cooking. Cool slightly, then purée in a food processor until smooth. Cool, then spread over the cooked shortbread.

4 Melt the chocolate in a heatproof bowl set over a saucepan of simmering water. Alternatively, melt the chocolate in the microwave according to the manufacturer's instructions. Stir until smooth, then spread over the top of the fig filling. Leave to become firm, then cut into 12 bars and serve.

INGREDIENTS
Makes 12

1 stick butter
1¼ cups all-purpose flour
¼ cup firmly packed golden brown sugar
1⅓ cups dried figs, halved
2 tbsp. lemon juice
1 tsp. ground cinnamon
4 squares unsweetened chocolate

Helpful Hint

If you are unable to find ready-to-eat figs, soak dried figs in boiling water for 20 minutes until plump. Drain well and use as above.

Chocolate-Covered Pan Cake

1 Preheat the oven to 350° F. Lightly grease a 9 x 13 inch jelly-roll pan, and line with nonstick baking parchment. Place the flour, rolled oats, golden brown sugar, baking soda, and salt into a bowl, and stir together well.

2 Melt the butter and corn syrup together in a heavy saucepan and stir until smooth, then add to the oat mixture and mix together thoroughly. Spoon the batter into the prepared pan, and press down firmly.

3 Bake in the preheated oven for 15–20 minutes or until golden. Remove from the oven and let the cake cool in the pan. Once cool, remove from the tin. Discard the parchment.

4 Melt the chocolate in a heatproof bowl set over a saucepan of gently simmering water. Alternatively, melt the chocolate in the microwave according to the manufacturer's instructions. Once the chocolate has melted, quickly beat in the cream, then pour over the cake. Mark patterns over the chocolate with a fork when almost set.

5 Chill the cake in the refrigerator for at least 30 minutes before cutting into bars. When the chocolate has set, serve. Store in an airtight container for a few days.

INGREDIENTS
Makes 24

1¾ cups all-purpose flour
1¼ cups rolled oats
1 cup firmly packed golden
    brown sugar
1 tsp. baking soda
pinch of salt
1¼ sticks butter
2 tbsp. corn syrup
9 squares unsweetened chocolate
5 tbsp. heavy cream

Helpful Hint

Try lightly greasing your measuring spoon before dipping it into the corn syrup. The syrup will slide off the spoon easily. Alternatively, warm the syrup slightly before measuring.

Shortbread Thumbs

1 Preheat the oven to 300° F. Lightly grease 2 baking sheets. Sift the flour into a large bowl, cut ¾ stick of the butter and the shortening into small cubes, add to the flour, then, using your fingertips, rub in until the batter resembles fine bread crumbs.

2 Stir in the granulated sugar, sifted cornstarch, and 4 tablespoons of unsweetened cocoa, and bring the batter together with your hand to form a soft and pliable dough.

3 Place on a lightly floured surface and shape into 12 small balls. Place onto the baking sheets at least 2 inches apart, then press each one with a clean thumb to make a dent.

4 Bake in the preheated oven for 20–25 minutes or until light golden brown. Remove from the oven and leave for 1–2 minutes to cool. Transfer to a wire rack and leave until cold.

5 Sift the confectioners' sugar and the remaining cocoa into a bowl, and add the remaining softened butter. Blend to form a smooth and spreadable frosting with 1–2 tablespoons of hot water. Spread a little frosting over the top of each cookie and place half a cherry on each. Allow to set before serving.

INGREDIENTS
Makes 12

1 cup self-rising flour
1 stick butter, softened
2 tbsp. shortening
¼ cup granulated sugar
¼ cup cornstarch, sifted
5 tbsp. unsweetened cocoa, sifted
1 cup confectioners' sugar
6 assorted colored candied cherries, rinsed, dried, and halved

Helpful Hint

After baking, remove the cooked cookies as soon as possible from the baking trays as they will continue to cook and could overcook. Cool completely on wire cooling racks before storing in airtight containers.

Food Fact

Using a combination of butter and shortening gives these cookies a softer texture than using all butter.

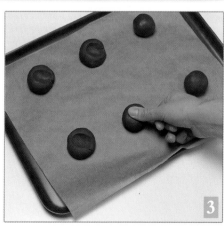

Checkered Cookies

1 Preheat the oven to 375° F. Lightly grease 3–4 cookie sheets. Place the butter and confectioners' sugar in a bowl, and cream together until light and fluffy.

2 Add the salt, then gradually add the flour, beating well after each addition. Mix well to form a firm dough. Cut the dough in half and knead the unsweetened cocoa into one half. Wrap both portions of dough separately in plastic wrap, and then let chill in the refrigerator for 2 hours.

3 Divide each piece of dough into 3 portions. Roll each portion of dough into a long roll, and arrange these rolls on top of each other to form a checkerboard design, sealing them with egg white. Wrap in plastic wrap and refrigerate for 1 hour.

4 Cut the dough into ¼-inch thick slices, place on the cookie sheets, and bake for 10–15 minutes. Remove from the oven, and let cool for a few minutes. Transfer to a wire rack and leave until cool before serving.

INGREDIENTS
Makes 20

1¼ sticks butter
¾ cup confectioners' sugar
pinch of salt
1¼ cups all-purpose flour
¼ cup unsweetened cocoa
1 small egg white

Helpful Hint

When baking cookies, use a spatula to transfer the cut-out cookies from the work surface to the cookie sheets. Use heavy-duty cookie sheets that will not bend or warp in the oven. The nonstick cookie sheets that are now readily available are ideal for baking cookies. Follow the manufacturer's instructions for greasing.

Food Fact

Recipes for sweet cookies and pastries often contain a pinch of salt. This helps to enhance the sweet flavor without making it savory.

Coconut & Almond Munchies

1 Preheat the oven to 300° F. Line several cookie sheets with rice paper. Place the egg whites in a clean, grease-free bowl, and beat until stiff and standing in peaks. Sift the confectioners' sugar, then carefully fold half of the sugar into the beaten egg whites together with the ground almonds. Add the coconut, the remaining confectioners' sugar, and the lemon rind, and mix together to form a very sticky dough.

2 Place the dough in a piping bag and pipe the dough into walnut-sized mounds onto the rice paper, then sprinkle with a little extra confectioners' sugar. Bake in the preheated oven for 20–25 minutes or until set and golden on the outside. Remove from the oven and let cool slightly. Using a spatula, carefully transfer to a wire rack until cool.

3 Break the semisweet and white chocolate into pieces and place in 2 separate bowls. Melt both chocolates set over saucepans of gently simmering water. Alternatively, melt in the microwave, according to the manufacturer's instructions. Stir until smooth and free from lumps. Dip one edge of each munchie in the semisweet chocolate and let dry on nonstick baking parchment. When dry, dip the other side into the white chocolate. Allow to set, then serve as soon as possible.

INGREDIENTS
Makes 26–30

5 medium egg whites
2¼ cups confectioners' sugar, plus extra to sprinkle
2 cups ground almonds
1¾ cups dried coconut
1 tbsp. grated lemon rind
4 squares semisweet chocolate
4 squares white chocolate

Helpful Hint

You could, if preferred, drop spoonfuls of this dough onto the rice paper. However, piping the dough ensures that the munchies will be more evenly sized.

Honey & Chocolate Hearts

1 Preheat the oven to 425° F. Lightly grease 2 cookie sheets. Heat the sugar, butter, and honey together in a small saucepan until everything has melted and the mixture is completely smooth.

2 Remove from the heat and stir until slightly cooled, then add the beaten egg with the salt and beat well. Stir in the mixed peel or candied ginger, ground cinnamon, ground cloves, flour, and baking powder, and mix until a dough is formed. Wrap in plastic wrap and chill in the refrigerator for 45 minutes.

3 Place the chilled dough on a lightly floured surface, roll out to about ¼-inch thickness and cut out small heart shapes. Place onto the prepared cookie sheets and bake in the preheated oven for 8–10 minutes. Remove from the oven and let cool slightly. Using a spatula, transfer to a wire rack until cool.

4 Melt the chocolate in a heatproof bowl set over a saucepan of simmering water. Alternatively, melt the chocolate in the microwave according to the manufacturer's instructions until smooth. Dip one half of each cookie in the melted chocolate. Allow to set before serving.

INGREDIENTS
Makes about 20

4½ tbsp. sugar
1 tbsp. butter
⅓ cup thick honey
1 small egg, beaten
pinch of salt
1 tbsp. mixed peel or chopped candied ginger
¼ tsp. ground cinnamon
pinch of ground cloves
2 cups all-purpose flour, sifted
½ tsp. baking powder, sifted
3 squares semisweet chocolate

Helpful Hint

When cutting out the hearts, start at the outside edge working into the center, cutting out the cookies as close as possible to minimize waste. Press the trimmings lightly together and roll out once more. Discard any remaining dough as it will be tougher and give a heavier cookie that will break up easily.

Tasty Tip

Try different types of honey to vary the flavor of the cookies. Acacia honey, for example, is very mild, while heather honey has a more pronounced flavor.

Chocolate Orange Cookies

1 Preheat the oven to 400° F. Lightly grease several cookie sheets. Coarsely grate the chocolate and set aside. Beat the butter and sugar together until creamy. Add the salt, beaten egg, and half the orange zest, and beat again.

2 Sift the flour and baking powder, add to the bowl with the chocolate, and beat to form a dough. Shape into a ball, wrap in plastic wrap, and chill in the refrigerator for 2 hours.

3 Roll the dough out on a lightly floured surface to ¼-inch thickness and cut into 2-inch rounds. Place the rounds on the prepared cookie sheets, allowing room for expansion. Bake in the preheated oven for 10–12 minutes or until firm. Remove the cookies from the oven and let cool slightly. Using a spatula, transfer to a wire rack and let cool.

4 Sift the confectioners' sugar into a small bowl and stir in sufficient orange juice to make a smooth, spreadable frosting. Spread the frosting over the cookies, leave until almost set, then sprinkle on the remaining grated orange zest before serving.

INGREDIENTS
Makes 30

3½ squares unsweetened chocolate
1 stick butter
½ cup sugar
pinch of salt
1 medium egg, beaten
3 tbsp. grated orange zest
1¾ cups all-purpose flour
1 tsp. baking powder
1 cup confectioners' sugar
1–2 tbsp. orange juice

Helpful Hint

To get the maximum amount of juice from citrus fruits, heat the whole fruit in the microwave for about 40 seconds, then cool slightly before squeezing. Alternatively, roll the fruit on the table, pressing lightly before squeezing out the juice. It is important to add the orange juice gradually to the frosting mixture, because you may not need all of it to obtain a spreadable consistency.

Rum & Chocolate Squares

1 Preheat the oven to 350° F. Lightly grease several cookie sheets. Cream the butter, sugar, and salt together in a large bowl until light and fluffy. Add the egg yolks and beat well until smooth.

2 Sift together 1½ cups of the flour, the cornstarch, and the baking powder and add to the mixture. Mix well with a wooden spoon until a smooth and soft dough is formed.

3 Halve the dough and knead the unsweetened cocoa into one half and the rum and the remaining flour into the other half. Place the 2 batters in 2 separate bowls, cover with plastic wrap, and chill in the refrigerator for 1 hour.

4 Roll out both pieces of dough separately on a well-floured surface into 2 thin rectangles. Place one on top of the other, cut out squares, and place on the prepared cookie sheets.

5 Bake in the preheated oven, half with the chocolate uppermost and the other half rum-side up, for 10–12 minutes or until firm. Remove from the oven and let cool slightly. Using a spatula, transfer to a wire rack and let cool, then serve.

INGREDIENTS
Makes 14–16

1 stick butter
⅔ cup sugar
pinch of salt
2 medium egg yolks
2 cups all-purpose flour
½ cup cornstarch
¼ tsp. baking powder
2 tbsp. unsweetened cocoa
1 tbsp. rum

Tasty Tip

If you prefer, you could substitute rum flavoring for the rum in this recipe. However, you would need to reduce the amount to about 1 teaspoon.

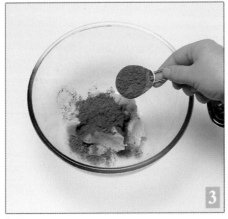

Chocolate Whirls

1 Preheat the oven to 350° F. Lightly grease 2 large baking sheets. Cream the butter and confectioners' sugar together in a large bowl until the batter is light and fluffy.

2 Stir the chocolate until smooth, then beat into the creamed batter. Stir in the cornstarch. Sift the flours together, then gradually add to the creamed batter, a little at a time, beating well between each addition. Beat until the consistency is smooth and stiff enough for piping.

3 Put the batter in a decorating bag fitted with a large star tip, and pipe 40 small whirls onto the baking sheets.

4 Bake the whirls in the preheated oven for 12–15 minutes or until firm to the touch. Remove from the oven and let cool for about 2 minutes. Using a spatula, transfer the whirls to wire racks and let cool.

5 Meanwhile, make the butter cream. Cream the butter with the vanilla extract until soft. Gradually beat in the confectioners' sugar and add a little cooled boiled water, if necessary, to give a smooth consistency.

6 When the chocolate whirls are completely cooled, pipe or spread on the prepared butter cream, sandwich together, and serve.

INGREDIENTS
Makes 20

1¾ sticks butter, softened
¾ cup confectioners' sugar, sifted
3 squares unsweetened chocolate, melted and cooled
2 tbsp. cornstarch, sifted
1 cup all-purpose flour
1 cup self-rising flour

FOR THE BUTTER CREAM:

1 stick unsalted butter, softened
½ tsp. vanilla extract
2 cups confectioners' sugar, sifted

Helpful Hint

It is important that the fat is at room temperature and the flours are sifted. Do not put too much batter into the decorating bag. If desired, the butter cream can be replaced with whipped cream, but the whirls should be eaten on the day they are filled.

Chunky Chocolate Muffins

1 Preheat the oven to 400° F. Line a muffin pan with 7 baking cups or grease the individual compartments well. Place the unsweetened chocolate in a large heatproof bowl set over a saucepan of very hot water, and stir occasionally until melted. Remove the bowl and let cool for a few minutes.

2 Stir the sugar and butter into the melted chocolate, then the milk, vanilla extract, and egg. Sift in the flour, baking powder, and salt together. Add the chopped white chocolate, then using a metal spoon, fold together quickly, taking care not to overmix.

3 Divide the batter among the baking cups, piling it up in the center. Bake on the center shelf of the preheated oven for 20–25 minutes or until well risen and firm to the touch.

4 Lightly dust the tops of the muffins with confectioners' sugar as soon as they come out of the oven, if desired. Leave the muffins in the pans for a few minutes, then transfer to a wire rack. Serve warm or cold.

INGREDIENTS
Makes 7

2 squares unsweetened chocolate, coarsely chopped
¼ cup golden brown sugar
¼ stick butter, melted
½ cup milk, heated to room temperature
½ tsp. vanilla extract
1 medium egg, lightly beaten
1¼ cups self-rising flour
½ tsp. baking powder
pinch of salt
3 squares white chocolate, chopped
2 tsp. confectioners' sugar (optional)

Helpful Hint

Measuring dry ingredients when baking is very important, as too much or too little of any ingredient can change the end result quite substantially. This applies especially to raising agents like baking powder, baking soda, and cream of tartar. It is a good idea to invest in a good set of measuring spoons, which are available in many of the larger department stores or in specialty stores for chefs.

Helpful Hint

If you do not have a large muffin pan, you can use a smaller muffin pan, in which case the quantities given will make 10–12 smaller muffins.

Fudgy Top Hat Chocolate Muffins

1 Preheat the oven to 375° F. Sift the flour, unsweetened cocoa, and baking powder into a bowl. Add the butter, sugar, egg, and milk. Beat for 2–3 minutes or until light and fluffy.

2 Divide the batter equally among 12 baking cups arranged in a muffin tray. Bake on the shelf above the center in the preheated oven for 15–20 minutes or until well risen and firm to the touch. Leave in the muffin pan for a few minutes, then transfer to a wire rack and let cool completely.

3 For the fudgy frosting, mix together the melted butter, milk, cocoa, and confectioners' sugar. Place a spoonful of frosting on the top of 6 of the buns, spreading out to a circle with the back of the spoon. Sprinkle with grated chocolate.

4 To make the top hats, use a sharp knife to cut and remove a circle of sponge about 1¼ inch across from each of the 6 remaining cakes. Whip the cream, orange liqueur, and 1 teaspoon of confectioners' sugar together until soft peaks form.

5 Spoon the filling into a decorating bag fitted with a large star tip, and pipe a swirl in the center of each cake. Replace the tops, then dust with the remaining confectioners' sugar and serve with the other muffins.

Helpful Hint

When grating chocolate, grate onto a piece of nonstick baking parchment using the coarse side of a box grater. It is then easier to sprinkle onto the muffins from the paper.

INGREDIENTS
Makes 12

½ cup self-rising flour
¼ cup unsweetened cocoa
½ tsp. baking powder
¾ stick butter, softened
¾ cup golden brown sugar
1 medium egg, lightly beaten
1 tbsp. milk

FOR THE FUDGY FROSTING:

1 tbsp. unsalted butter, melted
1 tbsp. milk
2 tbsp. unsweetened cocoa, sifted
3 tbsp. confectioners' sugar, sifted
1 square unsweetened chocolate, coarsely grated

FOR THE TOP HAT FILLING:

½ cup heavy cream
2 tsp. orange liqueur
1 tbsp. confectioners' sugar, sifted

Chocolate & Orange Rock Cookies

1 Preheat the oven to 400° F. Lightly grease 2 cookie sheets or line them with nonstick baking parchment. Sift the flour, unsweetened cocoa, and baking powder into a bowl. Cut the butter into small squares. Add to the dry ingredients, then, using your hands, rub in until the mixture resembles fine bread crumbs.

2 Add the granulated sugar, pineapple, apricots, and cherries to the bowl, and stir to mix. Lightly beat the egg together with the grated orange rind and juice. Drizzle the egg mixture over the dry ingredients and stir to combine. The batter should be fairly stiff but not too dry; add a little more orange juice, if needed.

3 Using 2 teaspoons, shape the batter into 12 rough heaps on the prepared cookie sheets. Sprinkle generously with the raw sugar. Bake in the preheated oven for 15 minutes, switching the cookie sheets around after 10 minutes. Leave on the cookie sheets for 5 minutes to cool slightly, then transfer to a wire rack to continue cooling. Serve warm or cold.

INGREDIENTS
Makes 12

1¾ cups self-rising flour
¼ cup unsweetened cocoa
½ tsp. baking powder
1 stick butter
3 tbsp. granulated sugar
⅓ cup candied pineapple, chopped
⅓ cup dried apricots, chopped
2 tbsp. candied cherries, quartered
1 medium egg
3 tsp. finely grated orange rind
1 tbsp. orange juice
2 tbsp. raw sugar

Helpful Hint

When making rock cookies it is important that you do not overmix the ingredients and do not add too much liquid, otherwise the "rocky" texture of the cookies will be lost. Vary the ingredients according to personal preference. If desired, add some nuts for extra crunch and texture. These cookies are best eaten within a day of being made, as they do not keep very well.

Rich Chocolate Cupcakes

1 Preheat the oven to 350° F. Line a 12-cup muffin pan with baking cups. Sift the flour and unsweetened cocoa into a bowl. Stir in the sugar, then add the melted butter, eggs, and vanilla extract. Beat together with a wooden spoon for 3 minutes or until well blended.

2 Divide half the batter among 6 of the paper cups. Dry the cherries thoroughly on absorbent paper towels, then fold into the remaining mixture and spoon into the rest of the paper cases.

3 Bake on the shelf above the center of the preheated oven for 20 minutes or until a toothpick inserted into the center of a cake comes out clean. Transfer to a wire rack until cool.

4 For the chocolate frosting, melt the chocolate and butter in a heatproof bowl set over a saucepan of hot water. Remove from the heat and let cool for 3 minutes, stirring occasionally. Stir in the confectioners' sugar. Spoon the mixture over the 6 chocolate cakes and allow to set.

5 For the cherry frosting, sift the confectioners' sugar into a bowl and stir in 1 tablespoon of boiling water, the butter, and cherry syrup. Spoon the frosting over the remaining 6 cakes, decorate each with a halved cherry, and allow to set.

INGREDIENTS
Makes 12

1½ cups self-rising flour
¼ cup unsweetened cocoa
¾ cup golden brown sugar
¾ stick butter, melted
2 medium eggs, lightly beaten
1 tsp. vanilla extract
2 tbsp. maraschino cherries, drained and chopped

FOR THE CHOCOLATE FROSTING:

2 squares unsweetened chocolate
¼ stick unsalted butter
¼ cup confectioners' sugar, sifted

FOR THE CHERRY FROSTING:

1 cup confectioners' sugar
2 tsp. unsalted butter, melted
1 tsp. syrup from the maraschino cherries
3 maraschino cherries, halved, to decorate

Tasty Tip

Do not expect the cakes to rise to the top of the cups; they should only come three-quarters of the way up and have fairly flat tops on which to spread the frosting.

Chocolate Madeleines

1 Preheat the oven to 350° F. Lightly grease 10 dariole molds and line the bottom of each with a small circle of nonstick baking parchment. Stand the molds on a baking sheet. Cream the butter and sugar together until light and fluffy. Gradually add the eggs, beating well between each addition. Beat in the almond extract and ground almonds.

2 Sift the flour, unsweetened cocoa, and baking powder over the creamed batter. Gently fold in using a metal spoon. Divide the batter equally among the prepared molds; each should be about half full.

3 Bake on the center shelf of the preheated oven for 20 minutes or until well risen and firm to the touch. Leave in the molds for a few minutes, then run a small palette knife around the edge and turn out onto a wire rack to cool. Remove the paper circles from the spongecakes.

4 Heat the jelly with the liqueur, brandy or juice in a small saucepan. Strain to remove any lumps. If necessary, trim the sponge bases, so they are flat. Brush the tops and sides with the warm jelly, then roll in the coconut. Top each with a chocolate button, fixed by brushing its bottom with a little of the jelly.

INGREDIENTS
Makes 10

1 stick butter
½ cup firmly packed golden brown sugar
2 medium eggs, lightly beaten
1 drop almond extract
1 tbsp. ground almonds
¾ cup self-rising flour
⅔ cup unsweetened cocoa
1 tsp. baking powder

TO FINISH:

5 tbsp. apricot jelly
1 tbsp. amaretto liqueur, brandy, or orange juice
½ cup dried coconut
10 large chocolate buttons or chips (optional)

Helpful Hint

Grease the molds well and dust with a little flour, shaking off any excess. Place a small circle of nonstick baking parchment in the bottom before filling to make removing the cooked cakes easier. Remove them as soon as possible after baking, as they have a tendency to stick.

Chocolate Chelsea Buns

1 Preheat the oven to 375° F. Lightly grease a 7-inch square pan. Place the pears in a bowl with the fruit juice, stir, then cover and let soak while making the dough.

2 Sift the flour, cinnamon, and salt into a bowl, rub in 2 tablespoons of the butter, then stir in the yeast and make a well in the center. Add the milk and egg, and mix to a soft dough. Knead on a floured surface for 10 minutes until smooth and elastic, then place in a bowl. Cover with plastic wrap and leave in a warm place to rise for 1 hour or until doubled in size.

3 Turn out on a lightly floured surface and knead the dough lightly before rolling out to a rectangle, about 9 x 12

inches. Melt the remaining butter and brush over. Spoon the pears and chocolate evenly over the dough, leaving a 1-inch border, then roll up tightly, starting at a long edge. Cut into 12 equal slices, then place cut-side up in the pan. Cover and allow to rise for 25 minutes or until doubled in size.

4 Bake on the center shelf of the preheated oven for 30 minutes or until well risen and golden brown. Cover with foil after 20 minutes if the filling is starting to brown too much.

5 Brush with the maple syrup while hot, then leave in the pan for 10 minutes to cool slightly. Turn out onto a wire rack and let cool. Separate the buns and serve warm.

INGREDIENTS
Makes 12

½ cup dried pears, finely chopped

1 tbsp. apple or orange juice

2 cups all-purpose flour

1 tsp. ground cinnamon

½ tsp. salt

3 tbsp. butter

1½ tsp. rapid-rise active dry yeast

½ cup warm milk

1 medium egg, lightly beaten

3 squares unsweetened chocolate, chopped

3 tbsp. maple syrup

Tasty Tip

As an alternative, replace the pears and juice with an equal amount of chopped hazelnuts or almonds.

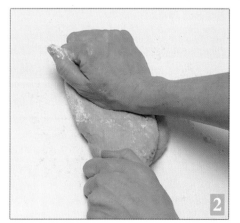

Fruit & Spice Chocolate Slice

1 Preheat the oven to 350° F. Grease and line a deep 7-inch square pan with nonstick baking parchment. Sift the flour and mixed spice into a large bowl. Cut the butter into small squares and, using your hands, rub in until the mixture resembles fine bread crumbs.

2 Add the chocolate, dried mixed fruit, apricots, and nuts to the dry ingredients. Set aside 1 tablespoon of the sugar, then add the rest to the bowl and stir together. Add the eggs and half of the milk and mix together, then add enough of the remaining milk to give a soft dropping consistency.

3 Spoon the batter into the prepared pan, level the surface with the back of a spoon, and sprinkle with the raw sugar. Bake on the center shelf of the preheated oven for 50 minutes. Cover the top with foil to keep the cake from browning too much, and bake for an additional 30–40 minutes or until it is firm to the touch and a toothpick inserted into the center comes out clean.

4 Leave the cake in the pan for 10 minutes to cool slightly, then turn out onto a wire rack and let cool completely. Cut into 10 slices and serve. Store in an airtight container.

INGREDIENTS
Makes 10 slices

3 cups self-rising flour

1 tsp. ground mixed spice

1½ sticks butter, chilled

4 squares unsweetened chocolate, coarsely chopped

⅔ cup dried mixed fruit

¾ cup dried apricots, chopped

¾ cup chopped mixed nuts

1½ cups raw sugar

2 medium eggs, lightly beaten

⅔ cup milk

Helpful Hint

When chopping dried apricots into small pieces, it is far easier if you use scissors, as dried apricots are sticky. Keep dipping the scissors into flour to keep the apricots from sticking together. This applies to all sticky ingredients, such as candied cherries, candied peel, and other dried fruits.

Helpful Hint

This cake is made by the rubbing-in method and will keep for several days wrapped in waxed paper, then in foil.

Chocolate Pecan Squares

1 Preheat the oven to 350° F. Lightly grease and line a 1 x 7 x 18 inch cake pan with nonstick baking parchment. Beat the butter and sugar together until light and fluffy. Sift in the flours and unsweetened cocoa, and mix together to form a soft dough.

2 Press the dough evenly over the base of the prepared pan. Prick all over with a fork, then bake on the shelf above the center of the preheated oven for 15 minutes.

3 Put the butter, sugar, corn syrup, milk, and vanilla extract in a small saucepan and heat gently until melted. Remove from the heat and let cool for a few minutes, then stir in the eggs and pour over the dough. Sprinkle with the nuts.

4 Bake in the preheated oven for 25 minutes or until dark golden brown but still slightly soft. Let cool in the pan. When cool, carefully remove from the pan, then cut into 12 squares and serve. Store in an airtight plastic container.

INGREDIENTS
Makes 12

1½ sticks butter
¾ cup confectioners' sugar, sifted
1½ cups all-purpose flour
¼ cup self-rising flour
¼ cup unsweetened cocoa

FOR THE PECAN TOPPING:

¾ stick butter
¼ cup golden brown sugar
2 tbsp. corn syrup
2 tbsp. milk
1 tsp. vanilla extract
2 medium eggs, lightly beaten
1 cup pecan halves

Helpful Hint

When a recipe calls for butter, the solid block variety (not the soft tub alternative, which has had air beaten in) must be used. Low-fat spreads break down when heated, and, as they contain a large proportion of water, the end result will be affected.

Tasty Tip

Pecans are perfect in this recipe, but if they are unavailable, substitute walnut halves instead.

Chocolate Brazil Nut & Polenta Squares

1 Preheat the oven to 350° F. Grease and line a deep 7-inch square pan with nonstick baking parchment. Finely chop ½ cup of the Brazil nuts and set aside. Coarsely chop the remainder. Cream the butter and sugar together until light and fluffy. Gradually add the eggs, beating well between each addition.

2 Sift the flour, unsweetened cocoa, cinnamon, baking powder, and salt into the creamed batter and then gently fold in using a large metal spoon or spatula. Add the milk, polenta, and ¾ cup of the coarsely chopped Brazil nuts. Fold into the batter.

3 Turn the batter into the prepared pan, leveling the surface with the back of the spoon. Sprinkle ½ cup of finely chopped Brazil nuts over the top. Bake the cake on the center shelf of the preheated oven for 45–50 minutes or until well risen and lightly browned, and when a clean toothpick inserted into the center of the cake for a few seconds comes out clean.

4 Leave the cake in the pan for 10 minutes to cool slightly, then turn out onto a wire rack to cool completely. Cut the cake into 9 equal squares and serve. Store in an airtight container.

INGREDIENTS
Makes 9 squares

1¼ cups shelled Brazil nuts

1¼ sticks butter, softened

⅔ cup firmly packed golden brown sugar

2 medium eggs, lightly beaten

¾ cup all-purpose flour

¼ cup unsweetened cocoa

¼ tsp. ground cinnamon

1 tsp. baking powder

pinch of salt

⅓ cup milk

⅓ cup instant polenta

Tasty Tip

Check the cake after 35 minutes of cooking; if the nuts are starting to brown too much, loosely cover with foil and continue cooking.

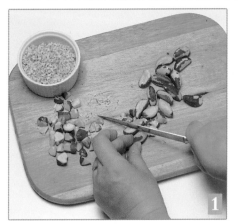

Moist Mocha & Coconut Cake

1 Preheat the oven to 325° F. Lightly grease and line a deep 8-inch square pan with nonstick baking parchment. Place the ground coffee in a small bowl and pour over the hot milk. Leave to infuse for 5 minutes, then strain through a strainer lined with cheesecloth. You will end up with about 4 tablespoons of liquid. Set aside.

2 Put the butter, corn syrup, sugar, and coconut in a small heavy saucepan and heat gently until the butter has melted and the sugar dissolved. Sift the flour, unsweetened cocoa, and baking soda together, and stir into the melted mixture with the eggs and 3 tablespoons of the coffee-infused milk.

3 Pour the batter into the prepared pan. Bake on the center shelf of the preheated oven for 45 minutes or until the cake is well risen and firm to the touch. Leave in the pan for 10 minutes to cool slightly, then turn out onto a wire rack to cool completely.

4 For the frosting, gradually add the confectioners' sugar to the softened butter, and beat together until mixed. Add the remaining 1 tablespoon of coffee-infused milk and beat until light and fluffy.

5 Carefully spread the coffee frosting over the top of the cake, then cut into 9 squares. Decorate each square with a small piece of chocolate flake and serve.

INGREDIENTS
Makes 9 squares

3 tbsp. ground coffee
⅔ cup hot milk
¾ stick butter
½ cup corn syrup
2 tbsp. firmly packed golden brown sugar
5 tbsp. dried coconut
1¼ cups all-purpose flour
¼ cup unsweetened cocoa
½ tsp. baking soda
2 medium eggs, lightly beaten
2 chocolate flakes, to decorate

FOR THE COFFEE FROSTING:

2 cups confectioners' sugar, sifted
1 stick butter, softened

Helpful Hint

It is important to use a very fine strainer to remove as much of the coffee as possible or the cake will have an unpleasant gritty texture.

Chocolate Walnut Squares

1 Preheat the oven to 325° F. Grease and line a 1 x 7 x 11 inch cake pan with nonstick baking parchment. Place the butter, chocolate, sugar, vanilla extract, and 1 cup of cold water in a heavy saucepan. Heat gently, stirring occasionally, until the chocolate and butter have melted, but do not allow to boil.

2 Sift the flours and unsweetened cocoa into a large bowl, and make a well in the center. Add the mayonnaise and about one-third of the chocolate mixture, and beat until smooth. Gradually beat in the remaining chocolate mixture.

3 Pour into the prepared pan and bake on the center shelf of the preheated oven for 1 hour or until slightly risen and firm to the touch. Place the pan on a wire rack and let cool. Remove the cake from the pan and peel off the baking parchment.

4 To make the chocolate glaze, place the chocolate and butter in a small saucepan with 1 tablespoon of water, and heat very gently, stirring occasionally until melted and smooth. Let cool until the chocolate has thickened, then spread evenly over the cake. Chill the cake in the refrigerator for about 5 minutes, then mark into 24 squares.

5 Lightly dust the walnut halves with a little confectioners' sugar, and place one on the top of each square. Cut into pieces and store in an airtight plastic container until ready to serve.

INGREDIENTS
Makes 24

1 stick butter
5 squares unsweetened chocolate, broken
2 cups sugar
½ tsp. vanilla extract
1¾ cups all-purpose flour
¾ cup self-rising flour
½ cup unsweetened cocoa
1 cup mayonnaise, at room temperature

FOR THE CHOCOLATE GLAZE:

4 squares unsweetened chocolate, broken
3 tbsp. unsalted butter
24 walnut halves
1 tbsp. confectioners' sugar, for dusting

Tasty Tip

Mayonnaise is used in this recipe instead of eggs. Make sure you use unflavored mayonnaise.

Nanaimo Bars

1 Grease and line a 1 x 7 x 11 inch cake pan with nonstick baking parchment. Place the butter and chocolate in a small heatproof bowl set over a saucepan of almost-boiling water until melted, stirring occasionally. Stir in the crumbs, coconut, and nuts into the chocolate mixture and mix well. Spoon into the prepared pan and press down firmly. Chill in the refrigerator for 20 minutes.

2 For the filling, place the egg yolk and milk in a bowl set over a saucepan of almost-boiling water, making sure the bowl does not touch the water. Beat for 2–3 minutes. Add the butter and vanilla extract and continue beating until fluffy, then gradually beat in the confectioners' sugar.

Spread over the chilled mixture, smoothing with the back of a spoon, and chill in the refrigerator for an additional 30 minutes.

3 For the topping, place the chocolate and corn oil in a heatproof bowl set over a saucepan of almost-boiling water. Melt, stirring occasionally until smooth. Let cool slightly, then pour over the filling and tilt the pan so that the chocolate spreads evenly.

4 Chill in the refrigerator for about 5 minutes or until the chocolate topping is just set but not too hard, then mark into 15 bars. Chill again in the refrigerator for 2 hours, then cut into slices and serve.

INGREDIENTS
Makes 15

¾ stick unsalted butter
4 squares unsweetened chocolate, coarsely chopped
1 cup graham cracker crumbs
¾ cup dried coconut
½ cup chopped mixed nuts

FOR THE FILLING:
1 medium egg yolk
1 tbsp. milk
¾ stick unsalted butter, softened
1 tsp. vanilla extract
1¼ cups confectioners' sugar

FOR THE TOPPING:
4 squares unsweetened chocolate, coarsely chopped
2 tsp. corn oil

Food Fact

These rich chocolate-topped squares originated in Nanaimo in British Columbia. Versions of this recipe are now popular all over Canada, including a version with a mint-flavored filling.

Marbled Toffee Shortbread

1 Preheat the oven to 350° F. Grease and line an 8-inch square cake pan with nonstick baking parchment. Cream the butter and sugar until light and fluffy, then sift in the flour and unsweetened cocoa. Add the semolina and mix together to form a soft dough. Press into the bottom of the prepared pan. Prick all over with a fork, then bake in the preheated oven for 25 minutes. Let cool.

2 To make the toffee filling, gently heat the butter, sugar, and condensed milk together until the sugar has dissolved. Bring to a boil, then simmer for 5 minutes, stirring constantly. Leave for 1 minute, then spread over the shortbread and let cool.

3 For the topping, place the different chocolates in separate heatproof bowls and melt one at a time, set over a saucepan of almost-boiling water. Drop spoonfuls of each on top of the toffee and tilt the pan to cover evenly. Swirl with a knife for a marbled effect.

4 Let the chocolate cool. When just set, mark into fingers using a sharp knife. Leave for at least 1 hour to harden before cutting into fingers.

INGREDIENTS
Makes 12

1½ sticks butter
½ cup sugar
1½ cups all-purpose flour
¼ cup unsweetened cocoa
½ cup fine semolina

FOR THE TOFFEE FILLING:

½ stick butter
¼ cup firmly packed golden brown sugar
14-oz. can condensed milk

FOR THE CHOCOLATE TOPPING:

3 squares unsweetened chocolate
3 squares semisweet chocolate
3 squares white chocolate

Helpful Hint

Make sure the toffee filling turns a rich golden color or it will not set. Cook for 3–4 minutes if necessary to obtain a good color. Take care that the mixture does not burn. If preferred, place the ingredients in a glass bowl and heat in the microwave on a medium setting in 30-second bursts until the sugar has melted; stir well after each burst of cooking. Once melted, heat on high for 2–4 minutes; again in 30-second bursts until golden.

Indulgent Chocolate Squares

1 Preheat the oven to 350° F. Grease and line a deep 8-inch square cake pan with nonstick baking parchment. Melt 8 squares of the unsweetened chocolate in a heatproof bowl set over a saucepan of almost-boiling water. Stir until smooth, then leave until just cool but not beginning to set.

2 Beat the butter and sugar until light and fluffy. Stir in the melted chocolate, ground almonds, egg yolks, unsweetened cocoa, and bread crumbs. Beat the egg whites until stiff peaks form, then stir a large spoonful into the chocolate mixture. Gently fold in the rest, then pour the batter into the prepared pan.

3 Bake on the center shelf in the preheated oven for 1¼ hours or until firm, covering the top with foil after 45 minutes to keep it from overbrowning. Leave in the pan for 20 minutes, then turn out onto a wire rack and let cool.

4 Melt the remaining 4 squares of unsweetened chocolate with the cream in a bowl set over a saucepan of almost boiling water, stirring occasionally. Let cool for 20 minutes or until thickened.

5 Spread the topping over the cake. Sprinkle with the white and semisweet chocolate and let set. Cut into 16 squares and serve decorated with freshly sliced strawberries, then serve.

INGREDIENTS
Makes 16

12 squares unsweetened chocolate

1½ sticks butter, softened

¾ cup firmly packed golden brown sugar

1½ cups ground almonds

6 large eggs, separated

3 tbsp. unsweetened cocoa, sifted

¾ cup fresh wheat bread crumbs

½ cup heavy cream

2 squares white chocolate, chopped

2 squares semisweet chocolate, chopped

freshly sliced strawberries, to decorate

Helpful Hint

To prevent the foil from coming off the top of the pan, especially in a convection oven, fold the foil around the edge, rather than simply laying it on top.

Fruit & Nut Refrigerator Fingers

1 Lightly grease and line the base of a 7-inch pan with nonstick baking parchment. Using greased kitchen scissors, snip each marshmallow into 4 or 5 pieces over a bowl. Add the dried mixed fruit, orange peel, cherries, and walnuts to the bowl. Sprinkle with the brandy and stir together. Add the crumbs and stir until mixed.

2 Break the chocolate into small pieces and put in a heatproof bowl with the butter set over a saucepan of almost-boiling water. Stir occasionally until melted, then remove from the heat. Pour the chocolate over the dry ingredients and mix well. Spoon into the prepared pan, pressing down firmly.

3 Chill in the refrigerator for 15 minutes, then mark into 12 fingers using a sharp knife. Chill in the refrigerator for an additional hour or until set. Turn out of the pan, remove the lining paper, and cut into fingers. Dust with confectioners' sugar before serving.

INGREDIENTS
Makes 12

14 pink and white marshmallows
½ cup luxury dried mixed fruit
3 tbsp. candied orange peel, chopped
3 tbsp. candied cherries, quartered
¾ cup walnuts, chopped
1 tbsp. brandy
2¼ cups graham cracker crumbs
8 squares unsweetened chocolate
1 stick unsalted butter
1 tbsp. confectioners' sugar, for dusting (optional)

Helpful Hint

Why not try storing nuts in the freezer? Stored this way, whole nuts will keep for 3 years, shelled nuts for 1 year, and ground nuts, such as ground almonds, for 3 months. Whole nuts will crack far easier when frozen, as their shells are far more brittle.

Helpful Hint

If you are using whole candied peel, rather than chopped, use kitchen scissors to cut it into small pieces.

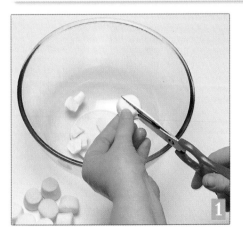

Crunchy-Topped Citrus Chocolate Slices

1 Preheat the oven to 325° F. Grease and line a 1 x 7 x 11 inch cake pan with nonstick baking parchment. Place the butter, sugar, and orange rind into a large bowl and cream together until light and fluffy. Gradually add the eggs, beating after each addition, then beat in the almonds.

2 Sift the flour and baking powder into the creamed batter. Add the grated chocolate and milk, then gently fold in using a metal spoon. Spoon the batter into the prepared pan.

3 Bake on the center shelf of the preheated oven for 35–40 minutes or until well risen and firm to the touch. Leave in the pan for a few minutes to cool. Turn out onto a wire rack and remove the baking parchment.

4 Meanwhile, to make the crunchy topping, place the sugar with the lime and orange juices into a small pitcher and stir together. Drizzle the sugar mixture over the hot cake, ensuring the whole surface is covered. Leave until completely cool, then cut into 12 slices and serve.

Helpful Hint

Store all dry ingredients, such as flour, baking powder, and sugar, in airtight containers in a cool, dry place.

Helpful Hint

It is important that the cake is still hot from the oven when the citrus topping is added, otherwise it will simply sit on the cake.

INGREDIENTS
Makes 12 slices

1½ sticks butter
¾ cup firmly packed golden brown sugar
1 tbsp. finely grated orange rind
3 medium eggs, lightly beaten
1 tbsp. ground almonds
1½ cups self-rising flour
¼ tsp. baking powder
4 squares unsweetened chocolate, coarsely grated
2 tsp. milk

FOR THE CRUNCHY TOPPING:
½ cup granulated sugar
3 tbsp. lime juice
2 tbsp. orange juice

All-in-One Chocolate Fudge Cakes

1 Preheat the oven to 350° F. Grease and line a 7 x 11 inch cake pan with nonstick baking parchment.

2 Place the brown sugar and butter in a large bowl, and sift in the flour, unsweetened cocoa, baking powder, and salt. Add the eggs and corn syrup, then beat with an electric whisk for 2 minutes, then add 2 tablespoons of warm water and beat for an additional minute.

3 Turn the batter into the prepared pan and level the top with the back of a spoon. Bake on the center shelf of the preheated oven for 30 minutes or until firm to the touch. Turn the cake out onto a wire rack to cool.

4 To make the topping, gently heat the sugar and evaporated milk in a saucepan, stirring frequently until the sugar has dissolved. Bring the mixture to a boil and simmer for 6 minutes, without stirring.

5 Remove the mixture from the heat. Add the chocolate and butter, and stir until melted and blended. Pour into a bowl and chill in the refrigerator for 1–2 hours or until thickened. Spread the topping over the cake, then sprinkle with the chopped fudge. Cut the cake into 15 squares before serving.

INGREDIENTS
Makes 15 squares

¾ cup firmly packed dark brown sugar
1½ sticks butter, softened
1¼ cups self-rising flour
¼ cup unsweetened cocoa
½ tsp. baking powder
pinch of salt
3 medium eggs, lightly beaten
1 tbsp. corn syrup

FOR THE FUDGE TOPPING:

¾ cup granulated sugar
⅔ cup evaporated milk
6 squares unsweetened chocolate, coarsely chopped
3 tbsp. unsalted butter, softened
1 cup fudge candies, finely chopped

Tasty Tip
Use a mixture of fudge candies for the topping on this cake, including chocolate, vanilla, and toffee flavors.

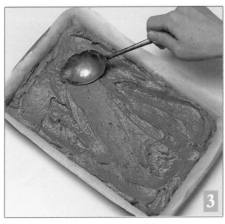

Marbled Chocolate Squares

1 Preheat the oven to 350° F. Grease and line a 1 x 7 x 11 inch cake pan with nonstick baking parchment. Cream the butter, sugar, and vanilla extract until light and fluffy. Gradually add the eggs, beating well. Sift in the flour and baking powder, and fold in with the milk.

2 Spoon half the batter into the prepared pan, spacing the spoonfuls apart and leaving gaps in between. Blend the unsweetened cocoa to a smooth paste with 2 tablespoons of warm water. Stir this into the remaining cake batter. Drop small spoonfuls between the vanilla cake batter to fill in all the gaps. Use a knife to swirl the batters together a little.

3 Bake on the center shelf of the preheated oven for 35 minutes or until risen and firm to the touch. Leave in the pan for 5 minutes to cool, then turn out onto a wire rack and let cool. Remove the baking parchment.

4 For the frosting, place the unsweetened and white chocolate in separate heatproof bowls and melt each over a saucepan of almost-boiling water. Spoon into separate nonstick baking parchment decorating bags, snip off the tips, and drizzle over the top. Allow to set before cutting into squares.

INGREDIENTS
Makes 18 squares

1½ sticks butter
¾ cup sugar
1 tsp. vanilla extract
3 medium eggs, lightly beaten
1¾ cups self-rising flour
½ tsp. baking powder
1 tbsp. milk
1½ tbsp. unsweetened cocoa

FOR THE CHOCOLATE FROSTING:

3 squares unsweetened chocolate, broken into pieces
3 squares white chocolate, broken into pieces

Tasty Tip

To marble the topping, spread the unsweetened chocolate evenly over the top of the cake. Put the white chocolate into a small decorating bag or a waxed paper decorating bag and drizzle over the unsweetened chocolate in random circles. Use a toothpick to drag the two chocolates together.

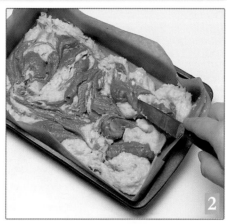

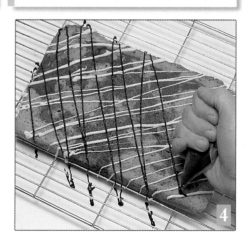

Triple Chocolate Brownies

1 Preheat the oven to 375° F. Grease and line 1 x 7 x 11 inch cake pan with nonstick baking parchment. Place the unsweetened chocolate in a heatproof bowl with the butter set over a saucepan of almost-boiling water, and stir occasionally until melted. Remove from the heat and leave until just cool but not beginning to set.

2 Place the sugar, eggs, vanilla extract, and coffee in a large bowl, and beat together until smooth. Gradually beat in the chocolate mixture. Sift the flour into the chocolate mixture. Add the pecans and the white and semisweet chocolate and gently fold in until mixed thoroughly.

3 Spoon the batter into the prepared pan and level the top. Bake on the center shelf of the preheated oven for 45 minutes or until just firm to the touch in the center and crusty on top. Let cool in the pan, then turn out onto a wire rack. Trim off the crusty edges and cut into 15 squares. Store in an airtight container.

INGREDIENTS
Makes 15

12 squares unsweetened chocolate, broken into pieces
2 sticks butter, cubed
1 cup sugar
3 large eggs, lightly beaten
1 tsp. vanilla extract
2 tbsp. very strong black coffee
¾ cup self-rising flour
1 cup pecans, coarsely chopped
3 squares white chocolate, coarsely chopped
3 squares semisweet chocolate, coarsely chopped

Food Fact

Brownies have a high proportion of sugar, giving the brownie its distinctive crusty topping. Underneath, the rich, gooey texture is produced by the small amount of flour used in comparison to the rest of ingredients.

Tasty Tip

Take care not to overcook; the outside crust should be crisp and the center of the brownies moist and gooey.

Light White Chocolate & Walnut Blondies

1 Preheat the oven to 375° F. Grease and line a 1 x 7 x 11 inch cake pan with nonstick baking parchment. Place the butter and raw sugar into a heavy saucepan and heat gently until the butter has melted and the sugar has started to dissolve. Remove from the heat and let cool.

2 Place the eggs, vanilla extract, and milk in a large bowl and beat together. Stir in the butter and sugar mixture, then sift in the 1 cup of flour, the baking powder, and salt. Gently stir the mixture twice.

3 Toss the walnuts and chocolate drops in the remaining 1 tablespoon of flour to coat. Add to the bowl and stir the ingredients together gently.

4 Spoon the batter into the prepared pan and bake on the center shelf of the preheated oven for 35 minutes or until the top is firm and crusty. Place the pan on a wire rack and let cool.

5 When completely cold, remove the cake from the pan and lightly dust the top with confectioners' sugar. Cut into 15 blondies, using a sharp knife, and serve.

INGREDIENTS
Makes 15

¾ stick unsalted butter

1 cup raw sugar

2 large eggs, lightly beaten

1 tsp. vanilla extract

2 tbsp. milk

1 cup all-purpose flour,
   plus 1 tbsp.

1 tsp. baking powder

pinch of salt

¾ cup walnuts, coarsely chopped

4 squares white chocolate drops

1 tbsp. confectioners' sugar

Tasty Tip

For a chocolate topping, mix together about ⅓ cup each of white, semisweet, and unsweetened chocolate chips. Sprinkle over the blondies as soon as they are removed from the oven. Let cool. Cut into squares and serve from the pan.

Nutty Date Cake with Chocolate Sauce

1 Lightly grease a 5-cup ovenproof bowl and line the bottom with a small circle of nonstick baking parchment. Cream the butter and sugar together in a large bowl until light and fluffy. Add the beaten eggs a little at a time, adding 1 tablespoon of the flour after each addition. When all the eggs have been added, stir in the remaining flour.

2 Add the grated chocolate and mix in lightly, then stir in the milk together with the hazelnuts and dates. Stir lightly until mixed together well.

3 Spoon the mixture into the prepared ovenproof bowl and level the surface. Cover with a double sheet of baking parchment with a pleat in the center, allowing for expansion, then cover either with a double sheet of foil, again with a central pleat. Secure with kitchen string.

4 Place in the top of a steamer, set over a saucepan of gently simmering water, and steam for 2 hours or until cooked and firm to the touch. Remember to add more water if necessary. Remove the cake from the saucepan and allow to rest for 5 minutes, then turn out onto a serving plate. Discard the small circle of baking parchment, then sprinkle with the chopped, toasted hazelnuts. Keep warm.

5 Meanwhile, make the sauce. Place the butter, sugar, and chocolate in a saucepan, and heat until the chocolate has melted. Stir in the cream and simmer for 3 minutes until thickened. Pour over the cake and serve.

INGREDIENTS
Serves 6–8

1 stick butter, softened
½ cup granulated sugar
3 medium eggs, beaten
1½ cups self-rising flour, sifted
2 squares unsweetened chocolate, grated
3 tbsp. milk
¾ cup hazelnuts, coarsely chopped
½ cup pitted dates, coarsely chopped
chopped toasted hazelnuts, to serve

FOR THE CHOCOLATE SAUCE:

½ stick unsalted butter
¼ cup firmly packed golden brown sugar
2 squares unsweetened chocolate, broken into pieces
½ cup heavy cream

Chocolate Brioche Bake

1 Preheat the oven to 350° F. Lightly grease an ovenproof dish. Melt the chocolate with 2 tablespoons of the butter in a small heatproof bowl set over a saucepan of simmering water. Stir until smooth.

2 Arrange half of the sliced brioche in the ovenproof dish, overlapping the slices slightly, then pour over half of the melted chocolate. Repeat the layers, finishing with a layer of chocolate.

3 Melt the remaining butter in a saucepan. Remove from the heat and stir in the orange oil or rind, the nutmeg, and the beaten eggs. Continuing to stir, add the sugar and finally the milk. Beat thoroughly and pour over the brioche. Let stand for 30 minutes before baking.

4 Bake on the center shelf in the preheated oven for 45 minutes or until the custard is set and the topping is golden brown. Let stand for 5 minutes, then dust with unsweetened cocoa and confectioners' sugar. Serve warm.

INGREDIENTS
Serves 6

7 squares unsweetened chocolate, broken into pieces
¾ stick unsalted butter
1 large brioche, sliced
1 tsp. pure orange oil or 1 tbsp. grated orange rind
½ tsp. freshly grated nutmeg
3 medium eggs, beaten
2 tbsp. raw sugar
2½ cups milk
unsweetened cocoa and confectioners' sugar, for dusting

Helpful Hint

Croissants, fruit buns, or fruit loaves are also suitable for this recipe. It is important that the dish is left to stand for 30 minutes before baking—do not omit this step.

Food Fact

Brioche is a type of French bread, enriched with eggs, butter, and sugar. It is available as a large round loaf, as a plait, in a long loaf shape, and also as individual buns. Any type is suitable for this recipe.

Mocha Pie

1 Place the prepared pastry shell on a large serving plate and set aside. Melt the chocolate in a heatproof bowl set over a saucepan of simmering water. Ensure the water is not touching the bottom of the bowl. Remove from the heat, stir until smooth, and let cool.

2 Cream the butter, brown sugar, and vanilla extract until light and fluffy, then beat in the cooled chocolate. Add the coffee, pour into the pastry shell, and chill in the refrigerator for about 30 minutes.

3 For the topping, beat the cream until beginning to thicken, then beat in the sugar and vanilla extract. Continue to beat until the cream is softly peaking. Spoon just under half of the cream into a separate bowl and fold in the dissolved coffee.

4 Spread the remaining cream over the filling in the pastry shell. Spoon the coffee-flavored whipped cream evenly over the top, then swirl it decoratively with a palate knife. Sprinkle with grated chocolate and chill in the refrigerator until ready to serve.

INGREDIENTS
Serves 4–6

1 sweet pastry shell or piecrust

FOR THE FILLING:
4 squares unsweetened chocolate, broken into pieces
1½ sticks unsalted butter
1 cup firmly packed brown sugar
1 tsp. vanilla extract
3 tbsp. strong black coffee

FOR THE TOPPING:
2 cups heavy cream
½ cup confectioners' sugar
2 tsp. vanilla extract
1 tsp. instant coffee dissolved in 1 tsp. boiling water, cooled
grated unsweetened and white chocolate, to decorate

Helpful Hint

Try storing well-wrapped brown sugar in the freezer. This will keep the sugar soft when thawed and prevent the sugar from sticking together in big lumps. If the sugar is already lumpy, soften in the microwave for a short time.

Helpful Hint

Using a ready-made pastry shell or pie crust makes this a quickly made pie that looks very impressive.

Individual Steamed Chocolate Desserts

1 Preheat the oven to 350° F. Lightly grease and line the bases of 8 individual ⅔-cup ovenproof bowls with a small circle of nonstick baking parchment. Cream the butter with ¼ cup of the sugar and the nutmeg until light and fluffy.

2 Sift the flour and unsweetened cocoa together, then stir into the creamed mixture. Beat in the egg yolks and mix well, then fold in the ground almonds and the bread crumbs.

3 Beat the egg whites in a clean, grease-free bowl until stiff and standing in peaks, then gradually beat in the remaining sugar. Using a metal spoon, fold a quarter of the egg whites into the chocolate mixture and mix well, then fold in the remaining egg whites.

4 Spoon the mixture into the prepared bowls, filling them two-thirds full to allow for expansion. Cover with a double sheet of foil and secure tightly with kitchen string. Stand the ovenproof bowls in a roasting pan and pour in enough water to come halfway up the sides of the bowls.

5 Bake in the center of the preheated oven for 30 minutes or until the desserts are firm to the touch. Remove from the oven, loosen around the edges, and invert onto warmed serving plates. Serve immediately with yogurt and chocolate curls.

INGREDIENTS
Serves 8

1¼ sticks unsalted butter, softened
¾ cup firmly packed golden brown sugar
½ tsp. freshly grated nutmeg
¼ cup all-purpose flour, sifted
4 tbsp. unsweetened cocoa, sifted
5 medium eggs, separated
1 cup ground almonds
½ cup fresh white bread crumbs

TO SERVE:
plain yogurt
orange-flavored chocolate curls

Helpful Hint

Look for individual plastic ovenproof bowls for making this recipe. They are very easy to unmold, as you simply squeeze them to release the pudding.

Chocolate Pear Pudding

1 Preheat the oven to 375° F. Butter an 8-inch round pan with 1 tablespoon of the butter and sprinkle the bottom with the brown sugar. Arrange the drained pear halves on top of the sugar, cut-side down. Fill the spaces between the pears with the walnut halves, flat-side up.

2 Cream the remaining butter with the granulated sugar, then gradually beat in the beaten eggs, adding 1 tablespoon of the flour after each addition. When all the eggs have been added, stir in the remaining flour.

3 Sift the unsweetened cocoa and baking powder together,

then stir into the creamed mixture with 1–2 tablespoons of the pear juice to give a smooth dropping consistency.

4 Spoon the mixture over the pear halves, smoothing the surface. Bake in the preheated oven for 20–25 minutes or until well risen and the surface springs back when lightly pressed.

5 Remove from the oven and let cool for 5 minutes. Using a palate knife, loosen the sides and invert onto a serving plate. Serve with custard sauce.

INGREDIENTS
Serves 6

1 stick butter, softened
2 tbsp. firmly packed brown sugar
14-oz. can of pear halves, drained
    and juice set aside
¼ cup walnut halves
½ cup golden granulated sugar
2 medium eggs, beaten
¾ cup self-rising flour, sifted
½ cup unsweetened cocoa
1 tsp. baking powder
prepared chocolate custard sauce,
    to serve

Helpful Hint

To soften butter quickly, pour hot water in a mixing bowl to warm, leave for a few minutes, then drain and dry. Cut the butter into small pieces and leave at room temperature for a short time. Do not attempt to melt in the microwave, as this will make the fat oily and affect the texture of the finished cake.

Tasty Tip

You could substitute fresh pears for the canned ones in this recipe. However, they would need to be poached first in a light syrup, otherwise they would discolor in the oven.

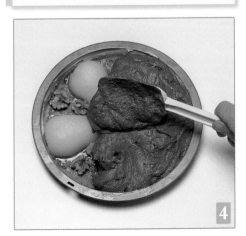

Peach & Chocolate Bake

1 Preheat the oven to 325° F, 10 minutes before baking. Lightly grease an 8-cup ovenproof dish.

2 Break the unsweetened chocolate and butter into small pieces, and place in a small heatproof bowl set over a saucepan of gently simmering water. Ensure the water is not touching the bottom of the bowl and leave to melt. Remove the bowl from the heat and stir until smooth.

3 Beat the egg yolks with the sugar until very thick and creamy, then stir the melted chocolate and butter into the beaten egg yolk mixture and mix together lightly.

4 Place the egg whites in a clean, grease-free bowl and beat until stiff, then fold 2 tablespoons of the beaten egg whites into the chocolate mixture. Mix well, then add the remaining egg white and fold in very lightly.

5 Fold the peach slices and the cinnamon into the mixture, then spoon the mixture into the prepared dish. Do not level the mixture, leave it a little uneven.

6 Bake in the preheated oven for 35–40 minutes or until well risen and just firm to the touch. Sprinkle the bake with the confectioners' sugar and serve immediately with spoonfuls of sour cream.

INGREDIENTS
Serves 6

7 squares unsweetened chocolate
1 stick unsalted butter
4 medium eggs, separated
½ cup sugar
15-oz. can peach slices, drained
½ tsp. ground cinnamon
1 tbsp. confectioners' sugar, sifted, to decorate
sour cream, to serve

Helpful Hint

As this cake contains no flour, it has a very dense texture. It is very important to fold the ingredients together very lightly, otherwise the air will be knocked out of the mixture.

Sticky Chocolate Surprise Cake

1 Preheat the oven to 350° F. Lightly grease an ovenproof soufflé dish. Sift the flour and unsweetened cocoa into a large bowl, and stir in the granulated sugar and the chopped mint-flavored chocolate. Make a well in the center.

2 Beat the milk, vanilla extract, and the melted butter together, then beat in the egg. Pour into the well in the dry ingredients and gradually mix together. Beat well until mixed thoroughly. Spoon into the prepared soufflé dish.

3 To make the sauce, blend the dark brown sugar and the unsweetened cocoa together and spoon over the top of the cake. Carefully pour the hot water over the top of the cake, but do not mix.

4 Bake in the preheated oven for 35–40 minutes or until firm to the touch and the mixture has formed a sauce underneath. Decorate with mint and serve immediately.

INGREDIENTS
Serves 6–8

1¼ cups self-rising flour
¼ cup unsweetened cocoa
1 cup granulated sugar
3 squares mint-flavored chocolate, chopped
¾ cup whole milk
2 tsp. vanilla extract
½ stick unsalted butter, melted
1 medium egg
sprig of fresh mint, to decorate

FOR THE SAUCE:
¾ cup firmly packed dark brown sugar
1 cup unsweetened cocoa
2½ cups hot water

Helpful Hint

All ovens vary, so it is important when baking to be aware of this. Always check the dish about 10 minutes before the end of the cooking time. If cooked, remove and make a note by the recipe. This is especially important if cooking with a convection oven, as they cook between 10–20 degrees hotter than conventional ovens. Most cakes are best if cooked in the center of the oven.

Food Fact

The surprise is that this dessert separates during cooking, creating a sticky chocolate cake with a chocolate custard sauce underneath.

Spicy White Chocolate Mousse

1 Tap the cardamom pods lightly so they split. Remove the seeds, then using a mortar and pestle, crush lightly. Pour the milk into a small saucepan and add the crushed seeds and the bay leaves. Bring to a boil gently over a medium heat. Remove from the heat, cover, and leave in a warm place for at least 30 minutes to infuse.

2 Break the chocolate into small pieces and place in a heatproof bowl set over a saucepan of gently simmering water. Ensure the water is not touching the bottom of the bowl. When the chocolate has melted, remove the bowl from the heat, and stir until smooth.

3 Whip the cream until it has slightly thickened and holds its shape but does not form peaks. Set aside. Beat the egg whites in a clean, grease-free bowl until stiff and standing in soft peaks.

4 Strain the milk through a strainer into the melted chocolate and beat until smooth. Spoon the chocolate mixture into the egg whites, then using a large metal spoon, fold gently. Add the whipped cream and fold in gently.

5 Spoon into a large serving dish or individual small cups. Chill in the refrigerator for 3–4 hours. Just before serving, dust with some unsweetened cocoa and then serve.

INGREDIENTS
Serves 4–6

6 cardamom pods
½ cup milk
3 bay leaves
7 squares white chocolate
1 cup heavy cream
3 medium egg whites
1–2 tsp. unsweetened cocoa, sifted, for dusting

Tasty Tip

Chocolate and spices go together very well, as this recipe demonstrates. White chocolate has an affinity with spices such as cardamom, while unsweetened and semisweet chocolate go very well with cinnamon.

Steamed Chocolate Chip Cake

1 Lightly grease an ovenproof bowl and line the bottom with a small circle of nonstick baking parchment. Sift the flour and baking powder into a bowl, add the bread crumbs, suet, and sugar, and mix well.

2 Stir in the eggs and vanilla extract with the chocolate chips, and mix with enough cold milk to form a smooth dropping consistency.

3 Spoon the mixture into the prepared bowl, and cover the cake with a double sheet of baking parchment and then a double sheet of foil with a pleat in the center to allow for expansion. Secure with kitchen string.

4 Place in the top of a steamer, set over a saucepan of simmering water, and steam for 1½–2 hours or until the pudding is cooked and firm to the touch—replenish the water as necessary. Remove and allow to rest for 5 minutes before turning out onto a warmed serving plate.

5 Meanwhile, make the custard sauce. Blend a little of the milk with the cornstarch and unsweetened cocoa to form a paste. Stir in the remaining milk with the sugar and vanilla extract. Pour into a saucepan and bring to a boil, stirring. Beat in the egg yolk and cook for 1 minute. Decorate the pudding with grated chocolate and serve with the sauce.

INGREDIENTS
Serves 6

1½ cups self-rising flour
½ tsp. baking powder
¾ cup fresh white bread crumbs
1 cup shredded suet
½ cup raw sugar
2 medium eggs, lightly beaten
1 tsp. vanilla extract
⅔ cup chocolate chips
⅔ cup cold milk
grated chocolate, to decorate

FOR THE CHOCOLATE CUSTARD SAUCE:

1¼ cups milk
1 tbsp. cornstarch
1 tbsp. unsweetened cocoa
1 tbsp. sugar
½ tsp. vanilla extract
1 medium egg yolk

Helpful Hint

The cornstarch in the custard helps to stabilize it, so if, when you are cooking the custard, it appears to begin curdling, remove it from the heat immediately and pour it into a clean bowl. Beat the custard sauce for 1–2 minutes, until it becomes smooth again.

Chocolate Fudge Sundae

1 To make the chocolate fudge sauce, place the chocolate and cream in a heavy saucepan and heat gently until the chocolate has melted into the cream. Stir until smooth. Mix the sugar with the flour and salt, then stir in sufficient chocolate mixture to make a smooth paste.

2 Gradually blend the remaining melted chocolate mixture into the paste, then pour into a clean saucepan. Cook over a low heat, stirring frequently until smooth and thick. Remove from the heat and add the butter and vanilla extract. Stir until smooth, then cool slightly.

3 To make the sundae, crush the raspberries lightly with a fork and set aside. Spoon a little of the chocolate sauce into the bottom of 2 sundae glasses. Add a layer of crushed raspberries, then a scoop each of vanilla and chocolate ice cream.

4 Top each one with a scoop of the vanilla ice cream. Pour over the sauce, sprinkle over the almonds, and serve with a wafer.

INGREDIENTS
Serves 2

FOR THE CHOCOLATE FUDGE SAUCE:
3 squares unsweetened chocolate, broken into pieces
2 cups heavy cream
¾ cup granulated sugar
¼ cup all-purpose flour
pinch of salt
1 tbsp. unsalted butter
1 tsp. vanilla extract

FOR THE SUNDAE:
1 cup raspberries, fresh or thawed if frozen
3 scoops vanilla ice cream
3 scoops homemade chocolate ice cream (see p. 116)
2 tbsp. toasted, slivered almond wafers, to serve

Helpful Hint

Store any remaining fudge sauce in the refrigerator for 1–2 weeks, warming it just before serving. Ice cream will keep for up to 2 months in the freezer if kept below 0° F. If using homemade ice cream, allow to soften in the refrigerator for at least 30 minutes before using.

Chocolate Ice Cream

1 Place the light cream and chocolate in a heavy saucepan, and heat gently until the chocolate has melted. Stir until smooth. Take care not to let the mixture boil. Remove from the heat.

2 Beat the eggs, egg yolks, and all but 1 tablespoon of the sugar together in a bowl until thick and pale.

3 Beat the warmed light cream and chocolate mixture with the vanilla extract into the custard mixture. Place the bowl over a saucepan of simmering water and continue beating until the mixture thickens and coats the back of a spoon. To test, lift the spoon out of the mixture and draw a clean finger through the mixture coating the spoon; if it leaves a clean line, then it is ready.

4 Stand the bowl in cold water to cool. Sprinkle the surface with the sugar to prevent a skin from forming while it is cooling. Whip the heavy cream until soft peaks form, then beat into the cooled chocolate custard.

5 Turn the ice-cream mixture into a rigid plastic container and freeze for 1 hour. Beat the ice cream thoroughly with a wooden spoon to break up all the ice crystals, then return to the freezer.

6 Continue to freeze for an additional hour, then remove and beat again.

7 Repeat this process once or twice more, then leave the ice cream in the freezer until firm. Allow to soften in the refrigerator for at least 30 minutes before serving.

8 Remove from the refrigerator, then sprinkle over the chopped nuts and grated chocolate, and serve with cherries.

INGREDIENTS
Makes 4 cups

2 cups light cream
7 squares unsweetened chocolate
2 medium eggs
2 medium egg yolks
½ cup sugar
1 tsp. vanilla extract
1 cup heavy cream

TO SERVE:
chopped nuts
coarsely grated white and
  unsweetened chocolate
a few cherries

Helpful hint

When beating the ice cream, expect it to melt a little. This is what should happen. Beating is necessary to break down any large ice crystals that have formed so that the finished ice cream is smooth rather than grainy or icy.

White Chocolate Trifle

1 Place the jelly-roll slices in the bottom of a trifle dish, and pour over the brandy, Irish cream liqueur, and a little of the black cherry juice to moisten the jelly roll. Arrange the black cherries on the top.

2 Pour 2 cups of the cream into a saucepan and add the white chocolate. Heat gently to just below the simmering point. Beat together the egg yolks, sugar, cornstarch, and vanilla extract in a small bowl.

3 Gradually beat the egg mixture into the hot cream, then strain into a clean saucepan and return to the heat.

4 Cook the custard gently, stirring throughout until thick.

5 Let the custard cool slightly, then pour over the trifle. Leave the trifle to chill in the refrigerator for at least 3–4 hours or preferably overnight.

6 Before serving, lightly whip the remaining cream until soft peaks form, then spoon the cream over the set custard. Using the back of a spoon, swirl the cream in a decorative pattern. Sprinkle with grated unsweetened and semisweet chocolate, and serve.

INGREDIENTS
Serves 6

1 chocolate jelly roll, sliced
4 tbsp. brandy
2 tbsp. Irish cream liqueur
15-oz. can black cherries, drained and pitted, with 3 tbsp. of the juice set aside
2½ cups heavy cream
4 squares white chocolate, broken into pieces
6 medium egg yolks
¼ cup sugar
2 tsp. cornstarch
1 tsp. vanilla extract
2 squares unsweetened chocolate, grated
2 squares semisweet chocolate, grated

Helpful Hint

It is critical that the custard is not allowed to boil once the eggs have been added, because then the mixture turns to sweet scrambled eggs and is unusable. Cook over a very gentle heat, stirring constantly and testing the mixture often.

White Chocolate Éclairs

1 Preheat the oven to 375° F. Lightly grease a baking sheet. Place the butter and ⅔ cup of water in a saucepan, and heat until the butter has melted, then bring to a boil.

2 Remove the saucepan from the heat and immediately add the flour all at once, beating with a wooden spoon until the mixture forms a ball in the center of the saucepan. Let cool for 3 minutes.

3 Add the eggs a little at a time, beating well after each addition until the paste is smooth, shiny, and of a piping consistency.

4 Spoon the mixture into a decorating bag fitted with a plain tip. Sprinkle the greased baking sheet with a little water. Pipe the mixture onto the baking sheet in 3-inch lengths, using a small, sharp knife to cut each pastry length neatly.

5 Bake in the preheated oven for 18–20 minutes or until well risen and golden. Make a slit along the side of each éclair to let the steam escape.

6 Return the éclairs to the oven for an additional 2 minutes to dry out. Transfer to a wire rack and let cool.

7 Halve the passion fruit, and using a small spoon, scoop the pulp of 4 of the fruits into a bowl. Add the cream, kirsch, and confectioners' sugar, and whip until the cream holds it shape. Spoon or pipe into the éclairs.

8 Melt the chocolate in a small heatproof bowl set over a saucepan of simmering water and stir until smooth.

9 Let the chocolate cool slightly, then spread over the top of the éclairs. Scoop the seeds and pulp out of the remaining passion fruit. Strain. Use the juice to drizzle around the éclairs when serving.

INGREDIENTS
Serves 4–6

½ stick unsalted butter
⅔ cup all-purpose flour, sifted
2 medium eggs, lightly beaten
6 ripe passion fruit
1 cup heavy cream
3 tbsp. kirsch
1 tbsp. confectioners' sugar
4 squares white chocolate, broken
  into pieces

Helpful Hint

Passion fruit are increasingly available in supermarkets. They are small, round, purplish fruits that should have quite wrinkled skins. Smooth ones are not ripe and will have little juice and poor flavor.

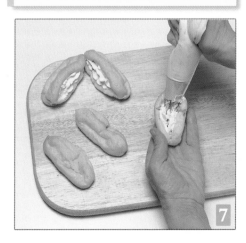

Chocolate Roulade

1 Preheat the oven to 350° F. Grease and line a 9 x 13 inch jelly-roll pan with a single sheet of nonstick baking parchment. Dust a large sheet of nonstick baking parchment with 2 tablespoons of the granulated sugar.

2 Place the egg yolks in a bowl with the remaining sugar, set over a saucepan of gently simmering water, and beat until pale and thick. Sift the unsweetened cocoa into the mixture and carefully fold in.

3 Beat the egg whites in a clean, grease-free bowl until soft peaks form. Gently add 1 tablespoon of the beaten egg whites into the chocolate mixture, then fold in the remaining whites. Spoon the batter into the prepared pan,

smoothing the batter into the corners. Bake in the preheated oven for 20–25 minutes or until risen and springy to the touch.

4 Turn the cooked roulade out onto the sugar-dusted baking parchment, and carefully peel off the lining paper. Cover with a clean, damp dishtowel and let cool.

5 To make the filling, pour the cream and whiskey into a bowl, and beat until the cream holds its shape. Grate in the chilled creamed coconut, add the confectioners' sugar, and gently stir in. Uncover the roulade and spoon about three-quarters of coconut cream on the roulade and roll up. Spoon the remaining cream on the top and sprinkle with the coconut, then serve.

INGREDIENTS
Serves 8

²⁄₃ *cup granulated sugar*
5 medium eggs, separated
½ *cup unsweetened cocoa*

FOR THE FILLING:
1 cup heavy cream
3 tbsp. whiskey
¼ *cup creamed coconut, chilled*
2 tbsp. confectioners' sugar
coarsely shredded coconut, toasted

Helpful Hint
Take care when rolling up the roulade in this recipe, as it can break up quite easily.

Chocolate Crepes

1 Preheat the oven to 400° F. To make the crepes, sift the flour, unsweetened cocoa, sugar, and nutmeg into a bowl, and make a well in the center. Beat the eggs and milk together, then gradually beat into the flour mixture to form a batter. Stir in ¼ cup of the melted butter and let stand for 1 hour.

2 Heat a 7-inch nonstick skillet and brush with a little melted butter. Add about 3 tablespoons of the batter and swirl to cover the bottom of the skillet. Cook over a medium heat for 1–2 minutes, flip over, and cook for an additional 40 seconds. Repeat with the remaining batter. Stack the crepes interleaving with waxed paper.

3 To make the sauce, place the mango, white wine, and sugar in a saucepan, and bring to a boil over a medium heat, then simmer for 2–3 minutes, stirring constantly. When the mixture has thickened, add the rum. Chill in the refrigerator.

4 For the filling, melt the chocolate and cream in a small, heavy saucepan over a medium heat. Stir until smooth, then let cool. Beat the egg yolks with the sugar for 3–5 minutes or until the mixture is pale and creamy, then beat in the chocolate mixture.

5 Beat the egg whites until stiff, then add a little to the chocolate mixture. Stir in the remainder. Spoon a little of the mixture onto a crepe. Fold in half, then fold in half again, forming a triangle. Repeat with the remaining crepes.

6 Brush the crepes with a little melted butter and bake in the preheated oven for 15–20 minutes or until the filling is set. Serve hot or cold with the mango sauce.

INGREDIENTS
Serves 6

FOR THE CREPES:
¾ cup all-purpose flour
1 tbsp. unsweetened cocoa
1 tsp. sugar
½ tsp. freshly grated nutmeg
2 medium eggs
¾ cup milk
¾ stick unsalted butter, melted

FOR THE MANGO SAUCE:
1 ripe mango, peeled and diced
¼ cup white wine
2 tbsp. granulated sugar
2 tbsp. rum

FOR THE FILLING:
8 squares unsweetened chocolate
⅓ cup heavy cream
3 eggs, separated
2 tbsp. granulated sugar

Chocolate Meringue Nest with Fruity Filling

1 Preheat the oven to 225° F, and line a baking tray with nonstick baking parchment. Place the hazelnuts and 2 tablespoons of the granulated sugar in a food processor, and blend to a powder. Add the chocolate and blend again until the chocolate is coarsely chopped.

2 In a clean, grease-free bowl, beat the egg whites and salt until soft peaks form. Gradually beat in the remaining sugar a teaspoonful at a time, and continue to beat until the meringue is stiff and shiny. Fold in the cornstarch and the white wine vinegar with the chocolate and hazelnut mixture.

3 Spoon the mixture into 8 mounds, about 4 inches in diameter, on the baking parchment. Make a hollow in each mound, then place in the preheated oven. Cook for 1½ hours, then switch the oven off and leave in the oven until cool.

4 To make the filling, whip the cream until soft peaks form. In another bowl, beat the mascarpone cheese until it is softened, then mix with the cream. Spoon the mixture into the meringue nests and top with the fresh fruits. Decorate with a few chocolate curls, and serve.

INGREDIENTS
Serves 8

1 cup hazelnuts, toasted
½ cup granulated sugar
3 squares unsweetened chocolate, broken into pieces
2 medium egg whites
pinch of salt
1 tsp. cornstarch
½ tsp. white wine vinegar
chocolate curls, to decorate

FOR THE FILLING:
½ cup heavy cream
⅔ cup mascarpone cheese
prepared summer fruits, such as strawberries, raspberries, and red currants

Helpful Hint

To make chocolate curls, melt the chocolate over hot water, then pour onto a cool surface, preferably marble if available. Leave until just set but not hard, then using a large cook's knife or a cheese parer, push the blade at an angle across the surface of the chocolate to form curls.

Triple Chocolate Cheesecake

1 Preheat the oven to 350° F. Lightly grease a 3 x 9 inch springform pan.

2 To make the base, mix together the crumbs and melted butter. Press into the bottom of the pan and allow to set. Chill in the refrigerator.

3 Place the white chocolate and cream in a small, heavy saucepan and heat gently until the chocolate has melted. Stir until smooth and set aside.

4 Beat the sugar and eggs together until light and creamy in color, add the cream cheese, and beat until the mixture is smooth and free from lumps.

5 Stir the white chocolate cream together with the cornstarch into the cream-cheese mixture.

6 Add the unsweetened and semisweet chocolate to the cream-cheese mixture, and mix lightly together until blended.

7 Spoon over the chilled base, place on a baking tray, and bake in the preheated oven for 1 hour.

8 Turn off the heat, open the oven door, and let the cheesecake cool in the oven. Chill in the refrigerator for at least 6 hours before removing the cheesecake from the pan. Cut into slices and transfer to serving plates. Serve with sour cream or plain yogurt.

INGREDIENTS
Serves 6

FOR THE BASE:
2 cups graham cracker crumbs
¼ stick butter, melted

FOR THE CHEESECAKE:
3 squares white chocolate, coarsely
  chopped
1 cup heavy cream
¼ cup sugar
3 medium eggs, beaten
14 oz. cream cheese
2 tbsp. cornstarch
3 squares unsweetened chocolate,
  coarsely chopped
3 squares semisweet chocolate,
  coarsely chopped
sour cream or plain yogurt,
  to serve

Helpful Hint

Leaving the cheesecake to cool in the oven helps to prevent cracks from forming on the top. However, do not worry if the top does crack—it will not affect the flavor of the cheesecake.

Fruity Chocolate Pudding with Sticky Chocolate Sauce

1 Lightly grease 4 individual ovenproof bowls, and sprinkle with a little of the dark brown sugar. Place a few orange segments in each bowl, followed by a spoonful of the cranberries.

2 Cream the remaining dark brown sugar with the soft butter until light and fluffy, then gradually beat in the eggs, a little at a time, adding 1 tablespoon of the flour after each addition. Sift the remaining flour, baking powder, and unsweetened cocoa together, then stir into the creamed mixture with 1 tablespoon of cooled boiled water to give a soft dropping consistency. Spoon the mixture into the bowls.

3 Cover each pudding with a double sheet of nonstick baking parchment with a pleat in the center and secure tightly with kitchen string. Cover with a double sheet of foil with a pleat in the center to allow for expansion and secure tightly with kitchen string. Place in the top of a steamer, set over a saucepan of gently simmering water, and steam steadily for 45 minutes or until firm to the touch. Remember to replenish the water if necessary. Remove the pudding from the steamer and allow to rest for about 5 minutes before running a knife around the edges of the puddings and turning out onto individual plates.

4 Meanwhile, make the chocolate sauce. Melt the chocolate and butter in a heatproof bowl set over a saucepan of gently simmering water. Add the sugar and corn syrup and stir until dissolved, then stir in the milk and continue to cook, stirring often until the sauce thickens. Decorate the puddings with a few chocolate curls and serve with the sauce.

INGREDIENTS
Serves 4

½ cup packed dark brown sugar
1 orange, peeled and segmented
¾ cup cranberries, fresh or thawed if frozen
1 stick butter, softened
2 medium eggs
¾ cup all-purpose flour
½ tsp. baking powder
3 tbsp. unsweetened cocoa
chocolate curls, to decorate

FOR THE STICKY CHOCOLATE SAUCE:

6 squares unsweetened chocolate, broken into pieces
½ stick butter
¼ cup sugar
2 tbsp. corn syrup
¾ cup milk

Helpful Hint

To make ahead, cook, unmold, then reheat on high in the microwave.

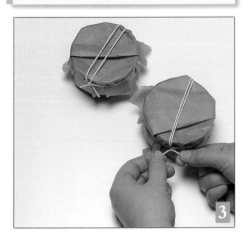

Chocolate Marshallow Pie

1 Preheat the oven to 350° F. Lightly grease a 7-inch cake pan.

2 Place the crackers in a plastic container, and crush finely with a rolling pin. Alternatively, place in a food processor and blend until fine crumbs are formed.

3 Melt the butter in a medium-sized saucepan, add the crumbs and mix together. Press into the bottom of the prepared pan and let cool in the refrigerator.

4 Melt 4 squares of the chocolate with the marshmallows and 2 tablespoons of water in a saucepan over a gentle heat, stirring constantly. Let cool slightly, then stir in the egg yolk, beat well, then return to the refrigerator until cool.

5 Beat the egg white until stiff and standing in peaks, then fold into the chocolate mixture.

6 Lightly whip the cream and fold three-quarters of the cream into the chocolate mixture. Set the remainder aside. Spoon the chocolate cream into the flan shell and chill in the refrigerator until set.

7 When ready to serve, spoon the remaining cream over the chocolate pie, swirling in a decorative pattern. Grate the remaining unsweetened chocolate and sprinkle over the cream, then serve.

INGREDIENTS
Serves 6

1¾ cups (about 18) graham crackers

¾ stick butter, melted

6 squares unsweetened chocolate

20 marshmallows

1 medium egg, separated

1 cup heavy cream

Tasty Tip

Replace the graham crackers with an equal amount of chocolate-covered cookies to make a quick change to this recipe.

Chocolate Rice Pudding Brûlée

1 Preheat the oven to 300° F. Preheat the broiler on high when ready to use. Gradually blend the unsweetened cocoa with 3 tablespoons of boiling water to form a soft, smooth paste. Place the rice, milk, bay leaf, orange zest, and the unsweetened cocoa paste in a saucepan. Bring to a boil, stirring constantly.

2 Reduce the heat and simmer for 20 minutes or until the rice is tender. Remove from the heat and discard the bay leaf, then add the white chocolate and stir until melted.

3 Beat together the granulated sugar and egg yolks until thick, then stir in the cream. Stir in the rice mixture together with the vanilla extract. Pour into a buttered, shallow dish. Stand the dish in a baking pan with sufficient hot water to come halfway up the sides of the dish.

4 Cook in the preheated oven for 1½ hours or until set. Stir occasionally during cooking, either removing the skin from the top or stirring the skin into the pudding. Remove from the pan and let cool.

5 When ready to serve, sprinkle the raw sugar over the surface of the rice pudding. Place under the preheated broiler, and cook until the sugar melts and caramelizes, turning the dish occasionally. Either serve immediately or chill in the refrigerator for 1 hour before serving.

INGREDIENTS
Serves 6

2 tbsp. unsweetened cocoa

⅓ cup short-grain rice

2½ cups milk

1 bay leaf

1 tbsp. grated orange zest

2 squares white chocolate, coarsely chopped

1 tbsp. granulated sugar

4 medium egg yolks

1 cup heavy cream

½ tsp. vanilla extract

4 tbsp. raw sugar

Tasty Tip

Short-grain rice is often labeled "pudding rice." The rice is short, quite fat, and pearly in appearance. It has a great deal of starch, which comes out of the rice during the long cooking and helps to make the finished dish very creamy.

Chocolate, Orange, & Pine Nut Tart

1 Preheat the oven to 400° F. Place the flour, salt, and sugar in a food processor with the butter and blend briefly. Add the egg yolks, 2 tablespoons of iced water, and the vanilla extract, and blend until a soft dough is formed. Remove and knead until smooth, wrap in plastic wrap, and chill in the refrigerator for 1 hour.

2 Lightly grease a 9-inch springform flan pan. Roll the dough out on a lightly floured surface to an 11-inch round, and use to line the pan. Press into the sides of the flan pan, crimp the edges, prick the bottom with a fork, and chill in the refrigerator for 1 hour. Bake blind in the preheated oven for

10 minutes. Remove and place on a large baking tray. Reduce the oven temperature to 375° F.

3 To make the filling, sprinkle the chocolate and the pine nuts evenly over the bottom of the pie crust. Beat the eggs, orange zest, Cointreau, and cream in a bowl until well blended, then pour over the chocolate and pine nuts.

4 Bake in the oven for 30 minutes or until the pastry is golden and the custard mixture is just set. Transfer to a wire rack to cool slightly. Heat the marmalade with 1 tablespoon of water and brush over the tart. Serve warm or at room temperature.

INGREDIENTS
Cuts into 8–10 slices

FOR THE SWEET PIECRUST:

1¼ cups all-purpose flour

½ tsp. salt

3–4 tbsp. confectioners' sugar

1 stick unsalted butter, diced

2 medium egg yolks, beaten

½ tsp. vanilla extract

FOR THE FILLING:

4 squares unsweetened chocolate, chopped

⅔ cup pine nuts, lightly toasted

2 large eggs

1 tbsp. grated orange zest

1 tbsp. Cointreau or orange-flavored liqueur

1 cup heavy cream

2 tbsp. orange marmalade

Food Fact

Cointreau is an orange-flavored liqueur and is used in many recipes. You could substitute Grand Marnier or any other orange liqueur, if you prefer.

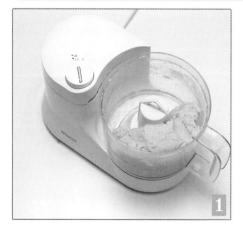

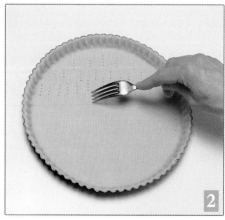

Chocolate Pecan Pie

1 Preheat the oven to 350° F. Roll the prepared dough out on a lightly floured surface and use to line a 10-inch pie plate. Roll the trimmings out and use to make a decorative edge around the pie, then chill in the refrigerator for 1 hour.

2 Set aside about 60 perfect pecan halves or enough to cover the top of the pie, then coarsely chop the remainder and set aside. Melt the chocolate and butter in a small saucepan over a low heat or in the microwave, and set aside.

3 Beat the eggs and brush the bottom and sides of the pie shell with a little of the beaten egg. Beat the sugar, corn syrup, and vanilla extract into the beaten eggs. Add the pecans, then beat in the chocolate mixture.

4 Pour the filling into the pie shell and arrange the pecan halves in concentric circles over the top. Bake in the preheated oven for 45–55 minutes or until the filling is well risen and just set. If the pastry edge begins to brown too quickly, cover with strips of foil. Remove from the oven and serve with ice cream.

INGREDIENTS
Cuts into 8–10 slices

1 cup prepared sweet piecrust dough (see p. 136)
1¼ cups pecan halves
4 squares unsweetened chocolate, chopped
¼ stick butter, diced
3 medium eggs
½ cup firmly packed brown sugar
½ cup corn syrup
2 tsp. vanilla extract
vanilla ice cream, to serve

Helpful Hint

Store chocolate in a cool, dark place. The best temperature to store it at is 68° F—if warmer, the chocolate will soften.

Helpful Hint

The pie shell in this recipe is not baked blind, but the pie does not become soggy because of the long cooking time, which allows the pastry to become crisp.

Pear & Chocolate Custard Tart

1 Preheat the oven to 375° F. To make the piecrust, put the butter, sugar, and vanilla extract into a food processor, and blend until creamy. Add the flour and unsweetened cocoa, and process until a soft dough forms. Remove the dough, wrap in plastic wrap, and chill in the refrigerator for at least 1 hour.

2 Roll out the dough between 2 sheets of plastic wrap to an 11-inch round. Peel off the top sheet of plastic wrap and invert the dough round into a lightly greased 9-inch springform cake pan, easing the dough into the bottom and sides. Prick the bottom with a fork, then chill for 1 hour.

3 Place a sheet of nonstick parchment paper and baking beans in the shell, and bake blind in the preheated oven for 10 minutes. Remove the baking parchment and beans, and bake for an additional 5 minutes. Remove and cool.

4 To make the filling, heat the chocolate, cream, and half the sugar in a medium saucepan over a low heat, stirring until melted and smooth. Remove from the heat and cool slightly before beating in the egg, egg yolk, and crème de cacao. Spread evenly over the bottom piecrust.

5 Peel the pears, then cut each pear in half and carefully remove the core. Cut each half crosswise into thin slices, and arrange over the custard sauce, gently fanning the slices toward the center and pressing into the chocolate custard sauce. Bake in the oven for 10 minutes.

6 Reduce the oven temperature to 350° F, and sprinkle the surface evenly with the remaining sugar. Bake in the oven for 20–25 minutes or until the custard is set and the pears are tender and glazed. Remove from the oven and let cool slightly. Cut into slices, then serve with spoonfuls of whipped cream.

INGREDIENTS
Cuts into 6–8 slices

FOR THE CHOCOLATE PIECRUST:
1 stick unsalted butter, softened
⅓ cup sugar
2 tsp. vanilla extract
1½ cups all-purpose flour, sifted
⅓ cup unsweetened cocoa
whipped cream, to serve

FOR THE FILLING:
4 squares unsweetened chocolate, chopped
1 cup heavy cream
¼ cup sugar
1 large egg
1 large egg yolk
1 tbsp. crème de cacao
3 ripe pears

Helpful Hint

The chocolate dough is very soft, so rolling it between sheets of plastic wrap will make it much easier to handle without having to add a lot of extra flour.

Double Chocolate Truffle Slice

1 Preheat the oven to 400° F. Prepare the chocolate piecrust and chill in the refrigerator, according to instructions.

2 Roll the dough out to a rectangle about 6 x 15 inches, and use to line a rectangular springform cake pan, trim the pastry, then chill in the refrigerator for 1 hour.

3 Place a sheet of nonstick parchment paper and baking beans in the pie shell, then bake blind in the preheated oven for 20 minutes. Remove the parchment paper and beans, and bake for 10 more minutes. Let the pie shell cool completely.

4 Bring the cream to a boil. Remove from the heat, and add the chocolate all at once, stirring until melted and smooth. Beat in the butter, then stir in the brandy or liqueur. Let cool slightly, then pour into the cooked pie shell. Refrigerate until set.

5 Cut out 1-inch strips of nonstick parchment paper. Place over the tart in a crisscross pattern, and dust with confectioners' sugar or cocoa.

6 Arrange chocolate leaves, caraque, or curls around the edges of the tart. Refrigerate until ready to serve. Allow to soften at room temperature for 15 minutes before serving.

INGREDIENTS
Cuts into 12–14 slices

*1 chocolate piecrust
  (see p. 140)*
1 cup heavy cream
*11 squares unsweetened chocolate,
  chopped*
2–3 tbsp. unsalted butter, diced
¼ cup brandy or liqueur
*confectioners' sugar or unsweetened
  cocoa, for dusting*

Tasty Tip

Liqueurs that would work very well in this recipe include Tia Maria, Kahlua, Cointreau, Grand Marnier, Amaretto, and Crème de Menthe.

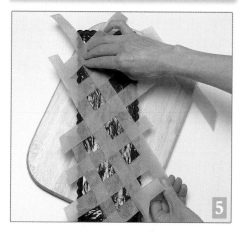

Double Chocolate Banana Pie

1 Preheat the oven to 375° F. Place the condensed milk in a heavy saucepan and place over a gentle heat. Bring to a boil, stirring constantly. Boil gently for about 3–5 minutes or until golden. Remove from the heat and let cool.

2 To make the ginger crumb crust, place the cookies with the melted butter, sugar, and ginger in a food processor, and blend together. Press into the sides and bottom of a 9-inch springform cake pan. Chill in the refrigerator for 15–20 minutes, then bake in the preheated oven for 5–6 minutes. Remove from the oven and let cool.

3 Melt the unsweetened chocolate in a medium-sized saucepan with ½ cup of the heavy cream, the corn syrup, and the butter over a low heat. Stir until smooth. Carefully pour into the crumb crust, tilting the pan to distribute the chocolate layer evenly. Chill in the refrigerator for at least 1 hour or until set.

4 Heat ½ cup of the remaining cream until hot, then add all the white chocolate and stir until melted and smooth. Stir in the vanilla extract and strain into a bowl. Let cool to room temperature.

5 Scrape the cooked condensed milk into a bowl and beat until smooth, adding a little of the remaining cream if too thick. Spread over the chocolate layer, then slice the bananas and arrange them evenly over the top.

6 Beat the remaining cream until soft peaks form. Stir a spoonful of the cream into the white chocolate mixture, then fold in the remaining cream. Spread over the bananas, swirling to the edge. Dust with a little unsweetened cocoa and chill the pie in the refrigerator until ready to serve.

INGREDIENTS
Cuts into 8 slices

2 14-oz. cans sweetened condensed milk

6 squares unsweetened chocolate, chopped

2 cups heavy cream

1 tbsp. corn syrup

¼ stick butter, diced

5 squares white chocolate, grated or finely chopped

1 tsp. vanilla extract

2–3 ripe bananas

unsweetened cocoa, for dusting

FOR THE GINGER CRUMB CRUST:

24–26 ginger cookies, coarsely crushed

1 stick butter, melted

1–2 tbsp. sugar, or to taste

½ tsp. ground ginger

Tasty Tip

Do not assemble the pie more than 2–3 hours before serving, as it will go too soft.

Chocolate Apricot Linzer Torte

1 Preheat the oven to 190° F. Lightly grease an 11-inch cake pan. Place the almonds and half the sugar into a food processor and blend until finely ground. Add the remaining sugar, flour, unsweetened cocoa, cinnamon, salt, and orange zest, and blend again. Add the diced butter and blend in short bursts to form coarse crumbs. Add the water, 1 tablespoon at a time, until the mixture starts to come together.

2 Turn onto a lightly floured surface, knead lightly, and roll out. Then using your fingertips, press half the dough onto the bottom and sides of the pan. Prick the bottom with a fork and chill in the refrigerator. Roll out the remaining dough between 2 pieces of plastic wrap to a 12 inch round. Slide the round onto a baking sheet and chill in the refrigerator for 30 minutes.

3 For the filling, spread the apricot jelly evenly over the chilled pie bottom and sprinkle with the chopped chocolate.

4 Slide the dough round onto a lightly floured surface and peel off the top layer of plastic wrap. Using a straight edge, cut the round into ½-inch strips; allow to soften until slightly flexible. Place half the strips about ½ inch apart to create a lattice pattern. Press down on each side of each crossing to accentuate the effect. Press the ends of the strips to the edge, cutting off any excess. Bake in the preheated oven for 35 minutes or until cooked. Let cool, then dust with confectioners' sugar. Serve cut into slices.

INGREDIENTS
Cuts into 10–12 slices

FOR THE CHOCOLATE ALMOND PIECRUST:
¾ cup whole blanched almonds
½ cup sugar
1¾ cups all-purpose flour
2 tbsp. unsweetened cocoa
1 tsp. ground cinnamon
½ tsp. salt
1 tbsp. orange zest
2 sticks unsalted butter, diced
2–3 tbsp. ice water

FOR THE FILLING:
1 cup apricot jelly
3 squares semisweet chocolate, chopped
confectioners' sugar, for dusting

Tasty Tip
When making the piecrust do not allow the dough to form into a ball or it will be tough.

Chocolate Peanut Butter Pie

1 Place the wafers or cookies, along with the melted butter, sugar, and vanilla extract, in a food processor and blend together. Press into the bottom of a 9-inch pie plate or cake pan. Chill in the refrigerator for 15–20 minutes.

2 Place 3 tablespoons of cold water in a bowl and sprinkle in the powdered gelatin. Leave until softened.

3 Blend half the sugar with the cornstarch, and salt in a heavy saucepan and gradually beat in the milk. Bring to a boil, then reduce the heat and boil gently for 1–2 minutes or until thickened and smooth, stirring constantly.

4 Beat all the egg yolks together, then beat in half of the hot milk mixture until blended. Beat in the remaining milk mixture, return to a clean saucepan, and cook gently until the mixture comes to a boil and thickens. Boil, stirring vigorously for 1 minute, then pour a quarter of the custard into a bowl. Add the chopped chocolate and rum or vanilla extract, and stir until the chocolate has melted and the mixture is smooth. Pour into the chocolate crust and chill in the refrigerator until set.

5 Beat the softened gelatin into the remaining custard and beat until thoroughly dissolved. Beat in the peanut butter until melted and smooth. Beat the egg whites until stiff, then beat in the remaining sugar, 1 tablespoon at a time.

6 Whip the cream until soft peaks form. Fold ½ cup of the cream into the custard, then fold in the egg whites. Spread the peanut butter cream mixture over the chocolate layer. Spread or pipe over the surface with the remaining cream, forming decorative swirls. Decorate with chocolate curls and chill in the refrigerator until ready to serve.

INGREDIENTS
Cuts into 8 slices

22–24 chocolate wafers or peanut butter cookies
1 stick butter, melted
1–2 tbsp. sugar
1 tsp. vanilla extract
1½ tbsp. gelatin
½ cup sugar
1 tbsp. cornstarch
½ tsp. salt
1 cup milk
2 large eggs, separated
2 large egg yolks
3½ squares unsweetened chocolate, chopped
2 tbsp. rum or 2 tsp. vanilla extract
½ cup smooth peanut butter
1 cup heavy cream
chocolate curls, to decorate

Mini Pistachio & Chocolate Strudels

1 Preheat the oven to 325° F. Lightly grease 2 large baking sheets. For the filling, mix the finely chopped pistachio nuts, sugar, and unsweetened chocolate in a bowl. Sprinkle with the rose water, stir lightly together, and set aside.

2 Cut each phyllo pastry sheet into 4 to make 7 x 9 inch rectangles. Place one rectangle on the work surface and brush with a little melted butter. Place another rectangle on top and brush with a little more butter. Sprinkle with a little sugar and spread about 1 spoonful of the filling along one short end. Fold the short end over the filling, then fold in the long edges and roll up. Place on the baking

sheet seam-side down. Continue with the remaining pastry sheets and filling until both are used.

3 Brush each strudel with the remaining melted butter, and sprinkle with a little sugar. Bake in the preheated oven for 20 minutes or until golden brown and the pastry is crisp.

4 Remove from the oven and leave on the baking sheet for 2 minutes, then transfer to a wire rack. Dust with confectioners' sugar. Place the melted white chocolate in a small decorating bag fitted with a plain writing pipe and pipe squiggles over the strudel. Let set before serving.

INGREDIENTS
Makes 24

5 large sheets phyllo pastry
½ stick butter, melted
1–2 tbsp. sugar, for sprinkling
2 squares white chocolate, melted, to decorate

FOR THE FILLING:

1 cup unsalted pistachios, finely chopped
3 tbsp. sugar
2 squares unsweetened chocolate, finely chopped
1–2 tsp. rose water
1 tbsp. confectioners' sugar, for dusting

Tasty Tip

Keep the unused phyllo pastry covered with a clean, damp dishtowel to prevent it from drying out.

Chocolate Mousse in Phyllo Cups

1 Preheat the oven to 350° F. Lightly grease 6 custard cups. Cut the phyllo pastry into 6-inch squares, place one square on the work surface, then brush with a little of the melted butter and sprinkle with a little sugar. Butter a second square and lay it over the first at an angle, sprinkle with a little more sugar, and repeat with two more pastry squares.

2 Press the assembled phyllo pastry into the greased custard cup, pressing into the bottom to make a flat base, while keeping the edges pointing up. Continue making the cups in this way, then place on a baking sheet, and bake in the preheated oven for 10–15 minutes or until crisp and golden. Remove and let cool before removing the phyllo cups. Leave until cool.

3 Melt the chocolate bars and milk in a small saucepan, stirring constantly until melted and smooth. Let cool for 10 minutes, stirring occasionally.

4 Whip the cream until thick and stir a spoonful into the melted chocolate bar mixture, then fold in the remaining cream. Beat the egg white until stiff, and fold into the chocolate bar mixture, along with the unsweetened cocoa. Chill the mousse in the refrigerator for 2–3 hours.

5 For the topping, boil ½ cup of the heavy cream, add the grated white chocolate and vanilla extract, and stir until smooth, then strain into a bowl and let cool. Beat the remaining cream until thick, then fold into the white chocolate cream mixture.

6 Spoon the mousse into the phyllo cups, cover with the cream mixture, and sprinkle with grated chocolate. Chill in the refrigerator before serving with chocolate sauce, if desired.

INGREDIENTS
Serves 6

6 large sheets phyllo pastry, thawed if frozen
3 tbsp. unsalted butter, melted
1 tbsp. sugar
3 chocolate bars, coarsely chopped
1½ tbsp. milk
1 cup heavy cream
1 large egg white
1 tsp. unsweetened cocoa
1 tbsp. unsweetened grated chocolate
chocolate sauce (see p. 158), to serve (optional)

FOR THE TOPPING:
1 cup heavy cream
4 squares white chocolate, grated
1 tsp. vanilla extract

Tasty Tip

When working with phyllo pastry, keep the dough that you are not using wrapped, so it does not dry out.

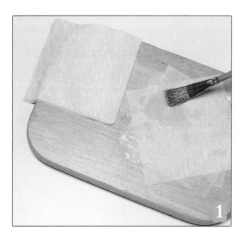

Raspberry Chocolate Ganache & Berry Tartlets

1 Preheat the oven to 400° F. Make the chocolate piecrust and use to line 8 3-inch tartlet pans. Bake blind in the preheated oven for 12 minutes.

2 Place ¾ cup of the cream and half of the raspberry jelly in a saucepan and bring to a boil, beating constantly to dissolve the jelly. Remove from the heat and add the chocolate all at once, stirring until the chocolate has melted.

3 Pour into the pastry-lined tartlet pans, shaking gently to distribute the ganache evenly. Chill in the refrigerator for 1 hour or until set.

4 Place the berries in a large, shallow bowl. Heat the remaining raspberry jelly with half the framboise liqueur over a medium heat until melted and bubbling. Drizzle over the berries and toss gently to coat.

5 Divide the berries among the tartlets, piling them up if necessary. Chill in the refrigerator until ready to serve.

6 Remove the tartlets from the refrigerator for at least 30 minutes before serving. Using an electric whisk, beat the remaining cream with the sugar and the remaining framboise liqueur until it is thick and softly peaking. Serve with the tartlets and sour cream.

INGREDIENTS
Serves 8

1 chocolate piecrust (see p. 140)
2 cups heavy cream
¾ cup seedless raspberry jelly
8 squares unsweetened chocolate, chopped
6½ cups raspberries or other summer berries
¼ cup framboise liqueur
1 tbsp. sugar
sour cream, to serve

Tasty Tip

Substitute an equal quantity of white chocolate for the unsweetened chocolate, as raspberries go well with it.

White Chocolate & Macadamia Tartlets

1 Preheat the oven to 400° F. Roll the dough out on a lightly floured surface and use to line 10 3-inch tartlet pans. Line each pan with a small piece of foil and fill with baking beans. Arrange the tartlets on a baking sheet and bake blind in the preheated oven for 10 minutes. Remove the foil and baking beans, and let the pie shells cool.

2 Beat the eggs with the sugar until light and creamy, then beat in the corn syrup, the butter, cream, and vanilla or almond extract. Stir in the macadamia nuts. Sprinkle three quarters of the chopped white chocolate equally over the bottoms of the tartlet shells and divide the mixture among them.

3 Reduce the oven temperature to 350°F and bake the tartlets for 20 minutes or until the tops are puffy and golden, and the filling is set. Remove from the oven and let cool on a wire rack.

4 Carefully remove the tartlets from their pans and arrange closely together on the wire rack. Melt the remaining white chocolate, and using a teaspoon or a small paper decorating bag, drizzle the melted chocolate over the surface of the tartlets in a zigzag pattern. Serve the tartlets slightly warm or at room temperature.

INGREDIENTS
Makes 10

1 sweet piecrust (see p. 136)
2 medium eggs
¼ cup sugar
¾ cup corn syrup
3 tbsp. butter, melted
¼ cup heavy cream
1 tsp. vanilla or almond extract
2 cups unsalted macadamia nuts, coarsely chopped
5 squares white chocolate, coarsely chopped

Food Fact

Macadamia nuts come from Hawaii and are large, crisp, buttery flavored nuts. They are readily available from supermarkets.

Chocolatey Puffs

1 Preheat the oven to 425° F. Lightly grease a large baking sheet. To make the choux pastry, sift the flour and unsweetened cocoa together. Place 1 cup of water, the salt, sugar, and butter in a saucepan, and bring to a boil. Remove from the heat and add the flour mixture all at once, beating vigorously with a wooden spoon until the mixture forms a ball in the center of the saucepan. Return to the heat and cook for 1 minute, stirring, then allow to cool slightly.

2 Using an electric mixer, beat in 4 of the eggs, one at a time, beating well after each addition. Beat the last egg and add a little at a time until the dough is thick and shiny, and just falls from a spoon when tapped on the side of the saucepan.

3 Pipe or spoon 12 large puffs onto the prepared baking sheet, leaving space between them. Cook in the preheated oven for 30–35 minutes or until puffy and golden. Remove from the oven, slice off the top third of each bun, and return to the oven for 5 minutes to dry out. Remove and let cool.

4 For the filling, heat the chocolate with ½ cup of the heavy cream and 1 tablespoon of sugar, if desired, stirring until smooth. Let cool. Whip the remaining cream until soft peaks form, and stir in the crème de cacao, if desired. Quickly fold the cream into the chocolate, then spoon or pipe into the choux buns and place the lids on top.

5 Place all the ingredients for the chocolate sauce in a small, heavy saucepan and heat gently, stirring until the sauce is smooth. Remove from the heat and let cool, stirring occasionally until thickened. Pour over the puffs and serve immediately.

INGREDIENTS
Makes 12 large puffs

FOR THE CHOUX PASTRY:

1¼ cups all-purpose flour

2 tbsp. unsweetened cocoa

½ tsp. salt

1 tbsp. sugar

1 stick butter, cut into pieces

5 large eggs

FOR THE CHOCOLATE CREAM FILLING:

8 squares unsweetened chocolate, chopped

2 cups heavy cream

1 tbsp. sugar (optional)

2 tbsp. crème de cacao (optional)

FOR THE CHOCOLATE SAUCE:

8 squares unsweetened chocolate

1 cup heavy cream

½ stick butter, diced

1–2 tbsp. corn syrup

1 tsp. vanilla extract

Rice Pudding & Chocolate Tart

1 Preheat the oven to 400° F. Roll the chocolate dough out and use to line a 9-inch cake pan. Place a sheet of baking parchment and baking beans in the pan, and bake blind in the preheated oven for 15 minutes.

2 For the ganache, place the cream and corn syrup in a heavy saucepan, and bring to a boil. Remove from the heat and add the chocolate all at once, stirring until smooth. Beat in the butter and vanilla extract, pour into the baked pie shell, and set aside.

3 For the rice pudding, bring the milk and salt to a boil in a medium-sized saucepan. Split the vanilla pod and scrape the seeds into the milk. Add the vanilla pod, sprinkle in the rice, then bring to a boil. Reduce the heat and simmer until the rice is tender and the milk is creamy. Remove from the heat.

4 Blend the cornstarch and sugar together, then stir in 2 tablespoons of water to make a paste. Stir a little of the hot rice mixture into the cornstarch mixture, then stir the cornstarch mixture into the rice. Bring to a boil and cook, stirring constantly until thickened. Set the bottom of the saucepan into a bowl of iced water and stir until cooled and thickened. Spoon the rice pudding into the tart, smoothing the surface. Allow to set. Dust with unsweetened cocoa, decorate with a few blueberries and fresh mint sprigs, and serve.

INGREDIENTS
Serves 8

1 chocolate piecrust (see p. 140)
1 tsp. unsweetened cocoa, for dusting

FOR THE CHOCOLATE GANACHE:
1 cup heavy cream
1 tbsp. corn syrup
6 squares unsweetened chocolate, chopped
1 tbsp. butter
1 tsp. vanilla extract

FOR THE RICE PUDDING:
4 cups milk
½ tsp. salt
1 vanilla pod
½ cup long-grain rice
1 tbsp. cornstarch
2 tbsp. sugar

TO DECORATE:
fresh blueberries
sprigs of fresh mint

Helpful Hint
Baking beans are usually ceramic, and so hold the heat well and help to cook the pie shell. If you don't have ceramic baking beans, you can use rice or dried beans instead.

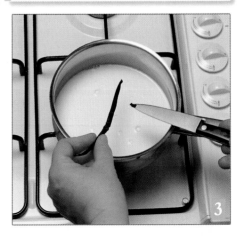

Chocolate Fruit Pizza

1 Preheat the oven to 400° F. Lightly grease a large baking sheet. Roll the prepared dough out to a 9-inch round, place the pastry round onto the baking sheet, and crimp the edges. Using a fork, prick the bottom all over, and chill in the refrigerator for 30 minutes.

2 Line the pie shell with foil and weigh down with an ovenproof, flat dinner plate or the bottom of a large cake pan, and bake blind in the preheated oven until the edges begin to brown. Remove from the oven, and discard the weight and foil.

3 Carefully spread the chocolate spread over the pizza bottom, and arrange the peach and nectarine slices around the outside edge in overlapping circles. Toss the berries with the unsweetened chocolate and arrange in the center. Drizzle with the melted butter and sprinkle with the sugar.

4 Bake in the preheated oven for 10–12 minutes or until the fruit begins to soften. Transfer the pizza to a wire rack.

5 Sprinkle the white chocolate and hazelnuts over the surface and return to the oven for 1 minute or until the chocolate begins to soften. If the pastry starts to darken too much, cover the edge with strips of foil. Remove to a wire rack and let cool. Decorate with sprigs of fresh mint and serve warm.

INGREDIENTS
Serves 8

1 sweet piecrust (see p. 136)
2 tbsp. chocolate spread
1 small peach, very thinly sliced
1 small nectarine, very thinly sliced
1¼ cups strawberries, halved or quartered
¾ cup raspberries
¾ cup blueberries
3 squares unsweetened chocolate, coarsely chopped
1 tbsp. butter, melted
2 tbsp. sugar
3 squares white chocolate, chopped
1 tbsp. hazelnuts, toasted and chopped
sprigs of fresh mint, to decorate

Helpful Hint

Alternatively, preheat the broiler and broil the pizza until the fruits begin to caramelize and the white chocolate begins to melt. Do not overheat, as the white chocolate could split and become gritty.

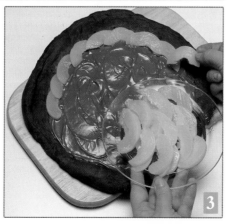

Chocolate Lemon Tartlets

1 Preheat the oven to 400° F. Roll the prepared dough out on a lightly floured surface and use to line 10 3-inch tartlet pans. Place a small piece of crumpled foil in each and bake blind in the preheated oven for 12 minutes. Remove from the oven and let cool.

2 Bring the cream to a boil, then remove from the heat and add the chocolate all at once. Stir until smooth and melted. Beat in the butter and vanilla extract, pour into the tartlets, and let cool.

3 Beat the lemon curd until soft, and spoon a thick layer over the chocolate in each tartlet, spreading gently to the edges. Do not chill in the refrigerator or the chocolate will be too firm.

4 Place the prepared custard sauce into a large bowl, and gradually beat in the cream and almond extract until the custard is smooth and runny.

5 To serve, spoon a little custard sauce onto a plate and place a tartlet in the center. Sprinkle with grated chocolate and almonds, then serve.

INGREDIENTS
Makes 10

1 sweet piecrust (see p. 136)

¾ cup heavy cream

6 squares unsweetened chocolate, chopped

2 tbsp. butter, diced

1 tsp. vanilla extract

1 cup lemon curd

1 cup prepared custard sauce

1 cup light cream

½–1 tsp. almond extract

TO DECORATE:

grated chocolate

toasted slivered almonds

Tasty Tip

Lemon curd is very easy to make. In a medium-sized heatproof bowl, mix together ¾ cup of sugar, 2 tablespoons lemon rind, 6 tablespoons lemon juice, and 4 large eggs. Add 1 stick cubed unsalted butter and place the bowl over a saucepan of gently simmering water. Stir often until thickened, about 20 minutes. Let cool and use as above.

Fudgy Mocha Pie
with Espresso Custard Sauce

1 Preheat the oven to 350° F. Line with foil or lightly grease a deep 9-inch pie plate. Melt the chocolate and butter in a small saucepan over a low heat and stir until smooth, then set aside. Dissolve the instant espresso powder in 1–2 tablespoons of hot water, and set aside.

2 Beat the eggs with the corn syrup, sugar, dissolved espresso powder, cinnamon, and milk until blended. Add the melted chocolate mixture and beat until blended. Pour into the pie plate.

3 Bake the pie in the preheated oven for about 20–25 minutes or until the edge has set but the center is still very soft. Let cool, remove from the plate, then dust lightly with confectioners' sugar.

4 To make the custard sauce, dissolve the instant espresso powder with 2–3 tablespoons of hot water, then beat into the prepared custard sauce. Slowly add the light cream, beating constantly, then stir in the coffee-flavored liqueur, if desired. Serve slices of the pie in a pool of espresso custard with strawberries.

INGREDIENTS
Cuts into 10 slices

4 squares unsweetened chocolate, chopped
1 stick butter, diced
1 tbsp. instant espresso powder
4 large eggs
1 tbsp. corn syrup
½ cup sugar
1 tsp. ground cinnamon
3 tbsp. milk
confectioners' sugar for dusting
fresh strawberries, to serve

FOR THE ESPRESSO CUSTARD SAUCE:
2–3 tbsp. instant espresso powder, or to taste
1 cup prepared custard sauce
1 cup light cream
2 tbsp. coffee-flavored liqueur (optional)

Helpful Hint

There are many brands of custard sauce available, including canned, and many supermarkets are now selling fresh custard sauce that can be found in the dairy section.

Chocolate Pecan Angel Pie

1 Preheat the oven to 225° F. Lightly grease a 9-inch pie plate.

2 Using an electric mixer, beat the egg whites and cream of tartar on a low speed until foamy, then increase the speed and beat until soft peaks form.

3 Gradually beat in the sugar, 1 tablespoon at a time, beating well after each addition, until stiff, glossy peaks form and the sugar is completely dissolved. (Test by rubbing a bit of meringue between your fingers—if gritty, continue beating.) This will take about 15 minutes.

4 Beat in 2 teaspoons of the vanilla extract, then fold in the nuts and the chocolate chips.

5 Spread the meringue evenly in the pie plate, making a shallow well in the center and slightly building up the sides.

6 Bake in the preheated oven for 1–1¼ hours or until a golden, creamy color. Lower the oven temperature if the meringue browns too quickly. Turn the oven off, but do not remove the meringue. Leave the oven door ajar, about 2 inches, for about 1 hour. Transfer to a wire rack until cool.

7 Pour the heavy cream into a small saucepan and bring to a boil. Remove from the heat, add the grated white chocolate, and stir until melted. Add the remaining vanilla extract and let cool, then whip until thick.

8 Spoon the white chocolate whipped cream into the pie shell, piling it high and swirling decoratively. Decorate with fresh raspberries and chocolate curls. Chill in the refrigerator for 2 hours before serving. When ready to serve, add sprigs of mint on the top and cut into slices.

INGREDIENTS
Cuts into 8–10 slices

4 large egg whites

¼ tsp. cream of tartar

1 cup sugar

3 tsp. vanilla extract

¾ cup pecans, lightly toasted and chopped

½ cup chocolate chips

½ cup heavy cream

5 squares white chocolate, grated

TO DECORATE:
fresh raspberries

unsweetened chocolate curls

few sprigs of fresh mint

Helpful Hint

The meringue needs to be cooked gently at a low temperature and allowed to cool in the oven, so that it can become crisp and dry without cracking too much.

Frozen Mississippi Mud Pie

1 Prepare the crumb crust and use to line a 9-inch springform cake pan and freeze for 30 minutes.

2 Soften the ice cream at room temperature for about 25 minutes. Spoon the chocolate ice cream into the crumb crust, spreading it evenly over the bottom, then spoon the coffee ice cream over the chocolate ice cream, mounding it slightly in the center. Return to the freezer to refreeze the ice cream.

3 For the topping, heat the unsweetened chocolate with the cream, corn syrup, and vanilla extract in a saucepan. Stir until the chocolate has melted and is smooth. Pour into a bowl and chill in the refrigerator, stirring occasionally, until cold but not set.

4 Spread the cooled chocolate mixture over the top of the frozen pie. Sprinkle with the chocolate and return to the freezer for 1½ hours or until firm. Serve at room temperature.

INGREDIENTS
Cuts 6–8 slices

1 ginger crumb crust (see p. 144)
2 cups chocolate ice cream
2 cups coffee-flavored ice cream

FOR THE CHOCOLATE TOPPING:
6 squares unsweetened chocolate, chopped
¼ cup light cream
1 tbsp. corn syrup
1 tsp. vanilla extract
2 squares coarsely grated white and semisweet chocolate

Helpful Hint

Use the best-quality ice cream that is available for this recipe. Look for chocolate ice cream with added ingredients such as chocolate chips, pieces of toffee, or rippled chocolate. If desired, you can add some raspberries, chopped nuts, or small pieces of chopped white chocolate to both the chocolate and coffee ice cream.

Tasty Tip

As an alternative, slice the frozen pie and serve with the chocolate topping while it is still hot.

White Chocolate Mousse & Strawberry Tart

1 Preheat the oven to 400° F. Roll the prepared dough out on a lightly floured surface and use to line a 10-inch cake pan.

2 Line with either foil or nonstick baking parchment and baking beans, then bake blind in the preheated oven for 15–20 minutes. Remove the foil or baking parchment and return to the oven for an additional 5 minutes.

3 To make the mousse, place the white chocolate with 2 tablespoons of water and ½ cup of the cream in a saucepan and heat gently, stirring until the chocolate has melted and is smooth. Remove from the heat, stir in the kirsch or framboise liqueur, and let cool.

4 Whip the remaining cream until soft peaks form. Fold a spoonful of the cream into the cooled white chocolate mixture, then fold in the remaining cream. If desired, beat the egg whites until stiff and gently fold into the white chocolate cream mixture to make a softer, lighter mousse. Chill in the refrigerator for 15–20 minutes.

5 Heat the strawberry jelly with the kirsch or framboise liqueur, and brush or spread half the mixture onto the bottom of the pie shell. Let cool.

6 Spread the chilled chocolate mousse over the jelly and arrange the sliced strawberries in concentric circles over the mousse. If necessary, reheat the strawberry jelly and glaze the strawberries lightly.

7 Chill the tart in the refrigerator for about 3–4 hours or until the chocolate mousse has set. Cut into slices and serve.

INGREDIENTS
Cuts into 10 slices

1 sweet piecrust (see p. 136)
¼ cup strawberry jelly
1–2 tbsp. kirsch or framboise liqueur
4–6 cups ripe strawberries, sliced lengthwise

FOR THE WHITE CHOCOLATE MOUSSE:
9 squares white chocolate, chopped
1½ cups heavy cream
3 tbsp. kirsch or framboise liqueur
1–2 large egg whites (optional)

Helpful Hint

This recipe contains raw egg whites, which should be eaten with caution by vulnerable groups including the elderly, young, and pregnant women. If you have concerns, omit them from the recipe.

Chocolate Raspberry Mille-Feuille

1 Preheat the oven to 400° F. Lightly grease a large baking sheet and sprinkle with a little water. Roll out the puff pastry on a lightly floured surface to a rectangle about 11 x 17 inches. Cut into 3 long strips. Mark each strip crosswise at 2½-inch intervals using a sharp knife; this will make cutting the baked puff pastry easier and neater. Carefully transfer to the baking sheet, keeping the edges as straight as possible.

2 Bake in the preheated oven for 20 minutes or until well risen and golden brown. Place on a wire rack and let cool. Carefully transfer each rectangle to a work surface, and using a sharp knife, trim the long edges straight. Cut along the knife marks to make 18 rectangles.

3 Place all the ingredients for the raspberry sauce in a food processor and blend until smooth. If the purée is too thick,

add a little water. Taste and adjust the sweetness if necessary. Strain into a bowl, cover, and chill in the refrigerator.

4 Place one pastry rectangle on the work surface flat-side down, spread with a little chocolate ganache, and sprinkle with a few fresh raspberries. Spread a second rectangle with a little ganache, place over the first, pressing gently, then sprinkle with a few raspberries. Place a third rectangle on top, flat-side up and spread with a little chocolate ganache.

5 Arrange some raspberries on top and dust lightly with a little confectioners' sugar. Repeat with the remaining pastry rectangles, chocolate ganache, and fresh raspberries.

6 Chill in the refrigerator until needed, and serve with the raspberry sauce and any remaining fresh raspberries.

INGREDIENTS
Serves 6

1 lb. puff pastry, thawed if frozen
1 quantity Chocolate Raspberry Ganache (see p. 154), chilled
6 cups fresh raspberries, plus extra for decorating
confectioners' sugar, for dusting

FOR THE RASPBERRY SAUCE:

2 cups fresh raspberries
2 tbsp. seedless raspberry jelly
1–2 tbsp. sugar, or to taste
2 tbsp. lemon juice or framboise liqueur

Helpful Hint

If you prefer, make one big mille-feuille by leaving the 3 strips whole in step 2. Slice the finished mille-feuille with a sharp serrated knife.

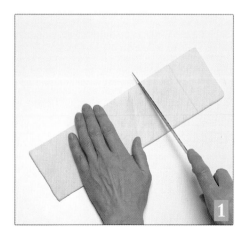

Chocolate Creams

1 Break the chocolate into small pieces, then place in a heatproof bowl set over a saucepan of gently simmering water. Add the brandy and heat gently, stirring occasionally until the chocolate has melted and is smooth. Remove from the heat and let cool slightly, then beat in the egg yolks, one at a time, beating well after each addition. Set aside.

2 Beat the egg whites until stiff but not dry, then stir 1 tablespoon into the chocolate mixture. Add the remainder and stir in gently. Chill in the refrigerator while preparing the cream.

3 Whip the cream until just beginning to thicken, then stir in the sugar, orange rind, and Cointreau, and continue to beat together until soft peaks form. Spoon the chocolate mousse into the cream mixture, and using a metal spoon, fold the 2 mixtures together to create a marbled effect. Alternatively, continue folding both mixtures together until mixed thoroughly. Spoon the mixture into four individual glass dishes, cover each dessert with a piece of plastic wrap, and chill in the refrigerator for 2 hours.

4 Using a potato peeler, shave the white chocolate into curls and sprinkle over the shavings. Top each dessert with a couple of cherries and then chill in the refrigerator until ready to serve.

INGREDIENTS
Serves 4

4 squares unsweetened chocolate

1 tbsp. brandy

4 medium eggs, separated

1 cup heavy cream

1 tbsp. sugar

1 tbsp. grated orange rind

2 tbsp. Cointreau or orange-flavored liqueur

1 square white chocolate

physalis or cherries,

to decorate

Food Fact

Physalis, although a delicious fruit, can be difficult to find in the United States. As suggested in the recipe, cherries work just as well, as do raspberries. Both taste delicious with chocolate.

Chocolate & Saffron Cheesecake

1 Preheat the oven to 400° F. Lightly grease an 8-inch fluted cake pan. Soak the saffron threads in 1 tablespoon of hot water for 20 minutes. Sift the flour and salt into a bowl. Dice the butter, then add to the flour. Using your fingertips, rub in the butter until the mixture resembles bread crumbs. Stir in the sugar.

2 Beat the egg yolk with 1 tablespoon of cold water, add to the mixture, and mix together until a smooth and pliable dough is formed. Add a little extra water if necessary. Knead on a lightly floured surface until free from cracks, then wrap in plastic wrap and chill in the refrigerator for 30 minutes.

3 Roll the pastry out on a lightly floured surface and use to line the cake pan. Prick the pie shell bottom and sides with a fork, and line with nonstick baking parchment and baking beans. Bake blind in the preheated oven for 12 minutes. Remove the baking beans and baking parchment, and continue to bake blind for 5 minutes.

4 Beat together the cottage cheese and granulated sugar, then add the melted chocolate, saffron liquid, milk, and eggs. Mix until blended thoroughly. Pour the mixture into the cooked flan shell and place on a cookie sheet.

5 Reduce the oven temperature to 375° F and bake for 15 minutes, then reduce the oven temperature to 350° F and continue to bake for 20–30 minutes or until set.

6 Remove the cheesecake from the oven and leave for 10 minutes before removing from the cake pan, if serving warm. If serving cold, leave in the cake pan to cool before removing and placing on a serving platter. Sprinkle with confectioners' sugar before serving.

INGREDIENTS
Serves 6

¼ tsp. saffron threads

1½ cups all-purpose flour

pinch of salt

¾ stick butter

1 tbsp. sugar

1 medium egg yolk

1½ cups cottage cheese

½ cup raw sugar

4 squares unsweetened chocolate, melted and cooled

6 tbsp. milk

3 medium eggs

1 tbsp. confectioners' sugar, sifted, to decorate

Food Fact

Saffron is the stamen of a particular type of crocus. It must be picked by hand and the yield is very small, making it very expensive. However, it is always used very sparingly and keeps very well.

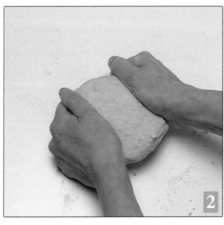

Caramelized Chocolate Tartlets

1 Preheat the oven to 400° F. Lightly grease six individual tartlet pans. Roll out the pastry on a lightly floured surface and use to line the greased pans. Prick the bottoms and sides with a fork, and line with nonstick baking parchment and baking beans. Bake blind for 10 minutes in the preheated oven, then remove from the oven, and discard the baking beans and the baking parchment.

2 Reduce the oven temperature to 350° F. Heat the coconut milk and 1 tablespoon of the sugar in a heavy saucepan, stirring constantly until the sugar has dissolved. Remove the saucepan from the heat and let cool.

3 Stir the melted chocolate, beaten egg, and vanilla extract into the cooled coconut milk. Stir until well mixed, then strain into the cooked pastry shells. Place on a baking sheet and bake in the oven for 25 minutes or until set. Remove and let cool, then chill in the refrigerator.

4 Preheat the broiler, then arrange the fruits in a decorative pattern on the top of each tartlet. Sprinkle with the remaining raw sugar and place the tartlets in the broiler pan. Broil for 2 minutes or until the sugar bubbles and browns. Turn the tartlets if necessary, and take care not to burn the sugar. Remove from the broiler and let cool before serving.

INGREDIENTS
Serves 6

1½ cups sweet piecrust, thawed if frozen

⅔ cup coconut milk

3 tablespoons raw sugar

2 squares unsweetened chocolate, melted

1 medium egg, beaten

few drops vanilla extract

1 small mango, peeled, pitted, and sliced

1 small papaya, peeled, seeded, and chopped

1 star fruit, sliced

1 kiwi, peeled and sliced, or use fruits of your choice

Helpful Hint

Before broiling, you may find it useful to cover the edges of the pastry with foil to prevent it burning under the hot broiler.

Hazelnut Meringues with Chocolate Sauce

1 Preheat the oven to 300° F. Line 2 baking sheets with nonstick baking parchment. Beat the egg whites in a large grease-free bowl until stiff, then add the sugar, 1 teaspoonful at a time, beating well after each addition. Continue to beat until the mixture is stiff and dry, then using a metal spoon, carefully fold in the ground hazelnuts.

2 Spoon the mixture into 12 quenelle shapes onto the baking parchment. Sprinkle over the ground hazelnuts, and bake in the preheated oven for 1½–2 hours or until dry and crisp. Turn the oven off and let cool in the oven.

3 To make the chocolate sauce, place the chocolate pieces with the butter, 4 tablespoons of the heavy cream, and the corn syrup in a small, heavy saucepan, and heat, stirring occasionally until the chocolate has melted and the mixture is blended. Do not let boil. Whip the remaining heavy cream until soft peaks form.

4 Sandwich the meringues together with the whipped cream and place on individual serving plates. Spoon over the sauce and serve with a spoonful of fresh mixed berries.

INGREDIENTS
Serves 6

4 medium egg whites
1 cup sugar
1 cup ground hazelnuts
½ cup toasted hazelnuts, sliced
fresh mixed berries, such as
*   raspberries, strawberries, and*
*   blueberries, to serve*

FOR THE CHOCOLATE SAUCE:

8 squares unsweetened chocolate,
*   broken into pieces*
½ stick butter
1 cup heavy cream
1 tbsp. corn syrup

Helpful Hint

It is important to add the sugar gradually when making meringues because if the sugar is not fully dissolved into the egg white, it might leach out during cooking, making the meringues "sweat."

Iced Chocolate & Raspberry Mousse

1 Break the ladyfingers into small pieces and divide among four individual glass dishes. Blend together the orange juice and Grand Marnier, then drizzle evenly over the ladyfingers. Cover with plastic wrap and chill in the refrigerator for about 30 minutes.

2 Meanwhile, place the cream in a small, heavy saucepan and heat gently, stirring occasionally until boiling. Remove the saucepan from the heat, then add the pieces of unsweetened chocolate and allow to stand untouched for about 7 minutes. Using a whisk, beat the chocolate and cream together until the chocolate has melted and is well blended and completely smooth. Let cool slightly.

3 Place the frozen raspberries and confectioners' sugar into a food processor or blender, and blend until coarsely crushed.

4 Fold the crushed raspberries into the cream and chocolate mixture and mix lightly until well blended. Spoon over the chilled ladyfingers. Lightly dust with a little unsweetened cocoa and decorate with whole raspberries, mint leaves, and grated white chocolate. Serve immediately.

INGREDIENTS
Serves 4

12 sponge ladyfingers
⅓ cup orange juice
2 tbsp. Grand Marnier or orange-flavored liqueur
1 cup heavy cream
6 squares unsweetened chocolate, broken into small pieces
2 cups frozen raspberries
6 tbsp. confectioners' sugar, sifted
unsweetened cocoa, for dusting

TO DECORATE:
fresh whole raspberries
mint leaves
grated white chocolate

Helpful Hint

Remove the raspberries from the freezer about 20 minutes before you need to purée them. This will soften them slightly, but they will still be frozen.

White Chocolate Terrine with Fruit Compote

1 Lightly grease and line a loaf pan with plastic wrap, taking care to keep the plastic wrap as wrinkle-free as possible. Break the white chocolate into small pieces, and place in a heatproof bowl set over a saucepan of gently simmering water. Leave for 20 minutes or until melted, then remove from the heat and stir until smooth. Let cool.

2 Whip the cream until soft peaks form. Beat the cream cheese until soft and creamy, then beat in the grated orange rind and ¼ cup of the sugar. Mix well, then fold in the whipped cream and then the cooled melted white chocolate.

3 Spoon the mixture into the prepared loaf pan and level the surface. Place in the freezer and freeze for at least 4 hours or until frozen. Once frozen, remember to return the freezer to its normal setting.

4 Place the fruit, along with the remaining sugar, in a heavy saucepan and heat gently, stirring occasionally until the sugar has dissolved and the juices from the fruit are just beginning to run. Add the Cointreau.

5 Dip the loaf pan into hot water for 30 seconds and invert onto a serving plate. Carefully remove the pan and plastic wrap. Decorate with sprigs of mint and serve sliced with the fruit compote.

INGREDIENTS
Serves 8

8 squares white chocolate
1 cup heavy cream
1 cup cream cheese
2 tbsp. finely grated orange rind
½ cup sugar
3 cups mixed summer fruits, such as strawberries, blueberries, and raspberries
1 tbsp. Cointreau or orange-flavored liqueur
sprigs of fresh mint, to decorate

Helpful Hint

Pour some boiled water into a tall pitcher and dip your knife into it for a few seconds. Dry the knife and use to slice the terrine, repeating the dipping when necessary.

Orange Chocolate Cheesecake

1 Lightly grease and line an 8-inch round springform cake pan with nonstick baking parchment. Place the cookies in a plastic container, and crush using a rolling pin. Alternatively, use a food processor. Melt the butter in a medium-sized heavy saucepan, add the crumbs, and mix well. Press the crumb mixture into the bottom of the lined pan, then chill in the refrigerator for 20 minutes.

2 For the filling, allow the cream cheese to come to room temperature. Place the cream cheese in a bowl and beat until smooth, then set aside.

3 Pour 4 tablespoons of water into a small bowl and sprinkle over the gelatin. Allow to stand for 5 minutes until spongy.

Place the bowl over a saucepan of simmering water and allow to dissolve, stirring occasionally. Let cool slightly.

4 Melt the orange chocolate in a heatproof bowl set over a saucepan of simmering water, then let cool slightly.

5 Whip the cream until soft peaks form. Beat the gelatin and chocolate into cream cheese. Fold in the cream. Spoon into the pan and level the surface. Chill in the refrigerator for 4 hours until set.

6 Remove the cheesecake from the pan and place on a serving plate. Top with the mixed fruits, dust with sifted confectioners' sugar, and decorate with sprigs of mint.

INGREDIENTS
Serves 8

1½ cups (about 18–20) chocolate-coated cookie crumbs
½ stick butter
4 cups mixed fruits, such as blueberries and raspberries
1 tbsp. confectioners' sugar, sifted
few sprigs of fresh mint, to decorate

FOR THE FILLING:
2 cups cream cheese
1 tbsp. gelatin
12 squares orange chocolate, broken into segments
2 cups heavy cream

Helpful Hint

Always add gelatin to the mixture you are working with and beat well to evenly distribute it. Never add the mixture to the gelatin or it will tend to set in a lump.

Chocolate Rice Pudding

1 Preheat the oven to 325° F. Lightly butter a large ovenproof dish. Rinse the rice, then place in the bottom of the buttered dish and sprinkle over the sugar.

2 Pour the evaporated milk and milk into a heavy saucepan and slowly bring to a boil over a low heat, stirring occasionally to avoid sticking. Pour the milk over the rice and sugar, and stir until well mixed and the sugar has dissolved.

3 Grate a little nutmeg over the top, then sprinkle with the ground cinnamon, if desired. Cover tightly with foil and bake in the preheated oven for 30 minutes.

4 Remove the pudding from the oven and stir well to break up any lumps that may have formed. Cover with foil and return to the oven for an additional 30 minutes. Remove the pudding from the oven once again and stir to break up any more lumps.

5 Stir the chocolate chips into the rice pudding and then dot with the butter. Continue to bake, uncovered, in the oven for an additional 45 minutes–1 hour or until the rice is tender and the skin is golden brown. Serve warm, with or without the skin, according to personal preference. Serve with a few sliced strawberries and a spoonful of sour cream.

INGREDIENTS
Serves 4

⅓ cup pudding or short-grain rice

⅓ cup sugar

14-oz. can evaporated milk

2½ cups milk

pinch of freshly grated nutmeg

¼ tsp. ground cinnamon (optional)

⅔ cup unsweetened chocolate chips

¼ stick butter

freshly sliced strawberries, to decorate

sour cream, to serve

Tasty Tip

If chocolate chips are unavailable, use a piece of unsweetened chocolate and chop it into small pieces.

Topsy Turvy Pudding

1 Preheat the oven to 350° F. Lightly grease an 8-inch deep round springform cake pan. Place the raw sugar and 3 tablespoons of water in a small, heavy saucepan, and heat gently until the sugar has dissolved. Swirl the saucepan or stir with a clean wooden spoon to ensure the sugar has dissolved, then boil rapidly until a golden caramel is formed. Pour into the bottom of the pan and let cool.

2 For the sponge, cream the butter and sugar together until light and fluffy. Gradually beat in the eggs a little at a time, beating well between each addition. Add a spoonful of flour after each addition to keep the batter from curdling. Add the chocolate and then stir well. Fold in the orange rind, self-rising flour, and the sifted unsweetened cocoa and mix well.

3 Remove the peel from both oranges, taking care to remove as much of the pith as possible. Thinly slice the peel into strips and then slice the oranges. Arrange the peel and then the orange slices over the caramel. Top with the sponge batter and level the top.

4 Place the pan on a baking sheet, and bake in the preheated oven for 40–45 minutes or until well risen, golden brown, and an inserted toothpick comes out clean. Remove from the oven, leave for about 5 minutes, invert onto a serving plate, and sprinkle with unsweetened cocoa. Serve with sour cream.

INGREDIENTS
Serves 6

FOR THE TOPPING:
¾ cup raw sugar
2 oranges

FOR THE SPONGE:
1½ sticks butter, softened
¾ cup sugar
3 medium eggs, beaten
1½ cups self-rising flour, sifted
2 squares unsweetened chocolate, melted
1 tbsp. grated orange rind
¼ cup unsweetened cocoa, sifted
sour cream, to serve

Helpful Hint

When making the caramel in step 1, make sure the sugar has completely dissolved and that no sugar remains clinging to the side of the pan, otherwise the caramel will crystallize.

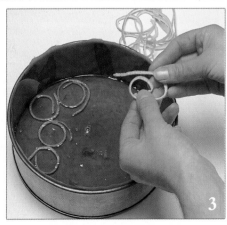

Chocolate Fruit Tiramisu

1 Cut the passion fruit, scoop out the seeds, and set aside. Plunge the nectarines or peaches into boiling water and leave for 2–3 minutes.

2 Carefully remove the nectarines from the water, cut in half, and remove the pits. Peel off the skin, chop the flesh finely, and set aside.

3 Break the sponge ladyfingers and amaretto cookies in half. Place the amaretto liqueur and prepared black coffee into a shallow dish and stir well. Place half the sponge ladyfingers and amaretto cookies into the amaretto and coffee mixture, and soak for 30 seconds.

4 Lift out both cookies from the liquor and arrange in the bottom of 4 deep individual glass dishes.

5 Cream the mascarpone cheese until soft and creamy, then slowly beat in the crème anglaise and mix well together.

6 Spoon half the mascarpone mixture over the cookies in the dishes and sprinkle with 4 squares of the finely chopped or grated unsweetened chocolate.

7 Arrange half the passion fruit seeds and the chopped nectarine or peaches over the chocolate, and sprinkle with half the sifted unsweetened cocoa.

8 Place the remaining cookies in the remaining coffee-liqueur mixture and soak for 30 seconds, then arrange on top of the fruit and unsweetened cocoa. Top with the remaining chopped or grated chocolate, nectarine or peach, and the mascarpone cheese mixture, piling the mascarpone high in the dishes.

9 Chill in the refrigerator for 1½ hours, then spoon the remaining passion fruit seeds and unsweetened cocoa over the desserts. Chill in the refrigerator for 30 minutes and serve.

INGREDIENTS
Serves 4

2 ripe passion fruit
2 fresh nectarines or peaches
¾ cup sponge ladyfingers
1 cup amaretto cookies
5 tbsp. amaretto liqueur
6 tbsp. prepared black coffee
1 cup mascarpone cheese
2 cups crème anglaise
7 squares unsweetened chocolate, finely chopped or grated
2 tbsp. unsweetened cocoa, sifted

Food Fact

Mascarpone cheese is an Italian cream cheese with a very thick, creamy texture. It is a classic ingredient of tiramisu. Here, it is mixed with a custard sauce, which gives it a lighter texture.

Fruity Chocolate Bread Pudding

1 Preheat the oven to 350° F. Lightly butter a shallow ovenproof dish. Break the chocolate into small pieces, then place in a heatproof bowl set over a saucepan of gently simmering water. Heat gently, stirring frequently until the chocolate has melted and is smooth. Remove from the heat and leave for about 10 minutes or until the chocolate begins to thicken slightly.

2 Cut the fruit loaf into medium to thick slices, then spread with the melted chocolate. Leave until almost set, then cut each slice in half to form a triangle. Layer the chocolate-coated bread slices and the chopped apricots in the buttered ovenproof dish.

3 Stir the cream and the milk together, then stir in the sugar. Beat the eggs, then gradually beat in the cream and milk mixture. Beat thoroughly until well blended. Carefully pour over the bread slices and apricots, and allow to stand for 30 minutes.

4 Sprinkle with the raw sugar and place in a roasting pan half filled with boiling water. Cook in the preheated oven for 45 minutes or until golden and the custard is lightly set. Serve immediately.

INGREDIENTS
Serves 4

6 squares unsweetened chocolate

1 small fruit loaf

¾ cup dried apricots, coarsely chopped

2 cups light cream

1¼ cups milk

1 tbsp. sugar

3 medium eggs

3 tbsp. raw sugar, for sprinkling

Helpful Hint

It is important to let the pudding stand for at least 30 minutes, as described in step 3. This allows the custard to soak into the bread—otherwise it sets around the bread as it cooks, making the pudding seem heavy.

Chocolate & Fruit Crumble

1 Preheat the oven to 375° F. Lightly grease an ovenproof dish.

2 For the crumble, sift the flour into a large bowl. Cut the butter into small dice and add to the flour. Rub the butter into the flour until the mixture resembles fine bread crumbs.

3 Stir the sugar, rolled oats, and the chopped hazelnuts into the mixture and set aside.

4 For the filling, peel the apples, core, and slice thickly. Place in a large, heavy saucepan with the lemon juice and 3 tablespoons of water. Add the golden raisins, raisins, and the brown sugar. Bring slowly to a boil, cover and simmer over a gentle heat for 8–10 minutes, stirring occasionally or until the apples are slightly softened.

5 Remove the saucepan from the heat, and let cool slightly before stirring in the pears, ground cinnamon, and the chopped chocolate.

6 Spoon into the prepared ovenproof dish. Sprinkle the crumble evenly over the top, then bake in the preheated oven for 35–40 minutes or until the top is golden. Remove from the oven, sprinkle with the sugar, and serve immediately.

INGREDIENTS
Serves 4

FOR THE CRUMBLE:
1 cup all-purpose flour

1 stick butter

¾ cup firmly packed golden brown sugar

½ cup rolled oats

½ cup hazelnuts, chopped

FOR THE FILLING:
1 lb. Granny Smith or other tart apples

1 tbsp. lemon juice

⅓ cup golden raisins

⅓ cup seedless raisins

¼ cup firmly packed golden brown sugar

¾ lb. pears, peeled, cored, and chopped

1 tsp. ground cinnamon

4 squares unsweetened chocolate, very coarsely chopped

2 tsp. sugar, for sprinkling

Tasty Tip

Granny Smith apples have a sharp flavor and may need more sugar than other apples. Their advantage is that they are ideal for cooking and will form a purée very easily. If you prefer, use a dessert apple such as Golden Delicious, but reduce the sugar accordingly.

Brandied Raisin Chocolate Mousse

1 Place the raisins in a bowl, along with the sugar, then pour over the brandy. Stir well and cover with plastic wrap. Allow to marinate overnight or until the raisins have absorbed most, or all, of the brandy. Stir occasionally during marinating.

2 Break the chocolate into small pieces and place in a small heatproof bowl set over a saucepan of gently simmering water. Heat gently, stirring occasionally, until the chocolate has melted and is smooth. Remove the bowl from the heat and allow to stand for about 10 minutes or until the chocolate cools and begins to thicken. Using a metal spoon or rubber spatula, carefully fold in the custard sauce.

3 Whip the cream until soft peaks form, and fold into the chocolate custard mixture with the coffee. Gently stir in the brandy-soaked raisins with any remaining brandy left in the bowl.

4 Beat the egg white in a clean, grease-free bowl until stiff but not dry, then fold 1 tablespoon into the chocolate mixture and mix together lightly. Add the remaining egg white and stir lightly until well mixed. Spoon into 4 tall glasses and chill in the refrigerator for 2 hours.

5 Just before serving, pipe a swirl of whipped cream on the top of each mousse and decorate with the chocolate curls.

INGREDIENTS
Serves 4

⅔ cup raisins
1 tsp. brown sugar
3 tbsp. brandy
7 squares unsweetened chocolate
⅔ cup custard sauce
1 cup heavy cream
1 tbsp. strong black coffee
1 medium egg white
¼ cup freshly whipped cream
chocolate curls, to decorate

Tasty Tip

Look for plump raisins that will soak up the alcohol really well.

Poached Pears with Chocolate Sauce

1 Pour the red wine with ⅔ cup of water into a heavy saucepan, and stir in the sugar, orange rind, and juice with ginger. Place over a gentle heat and bring slowly to a boil, stirring occasionally until the sugar has dissolved. Once the sugar has dissolved, boil steadily for 5 minutes, then remove from the heat.

2 Using a potato peeler, carefully peel the pears, leaving the stems intact. If desired, gently remove the cores from the bottom of each pear. (You can, if you prefer, leave the cores intact for a neater finish.) If necessary, cut a very thin slice off the bottom of each pear so they sit upright.

3 Carefully stand the pears in the hot syrup, return to the heat, cover with a lid, and simmer gently for 20 minutes or until tender, turning the pears occasionally. Remove from the heat and let cool in the syrup, turning occasionally. Using a slotted spoon, transfer the pears to a large dish.

4 Strain the syrup, then bring back to a boil and boil rapidly until reduced and syrupy. Add the chocolate, cream, and sugar to the saucepan and bring very slowly to a boil, stirring constantly until the chocolate has melted. Arrange the pears on serving plates and carefully spoon over the chocolate sauce. Serve immediately.

INGREDIENTS
Serves 4

1¼ cups red wine
½ cup sugar
1 tbsp. grated orange rind
1 tbsp. orange juice
1-in. piece fresh ginger, peeled and chopped
4 firm pears
6 squares unsweetened chocolate
½ cup heavy cream
2 tbsp. raw sugar

Tasty Tip

Look for pears that are ripe but not soft. You can use unripe pears. Conference pears have a green skin even when ripe and an elongated shape that makes them look very elegant.

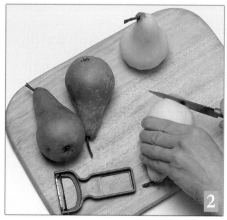

Chocolate Brûlée

1 Clean and hull the raspberries. Rinse lightly, then leave to dry on absorbent paper towels. Once dry, divide the raspberries evenly among 6 individual glass dishes.

2 Beat the sugar and egg yolks in a large bowl until very thick. Pour the cream into a heavy saucepan, place over a medium-high heat, and bring to a boil. Remove from the heat and gradually beat into the egg mixture, then beat in the vanilla extract.

3 Place the bowl over a saucepan of simmering water, and cook for about 15–20 minutes, stirring frequently or until thick and the custard coats the back of a wooden spoon.

4 Remove the bowl from the heat, add the chopped white chocolate, and stir until melted and well blended. Pour over the raspberries in the glass dishes and let cool. Cover with plastic wrap and chill in the refrigerator for 6 hours or until firm.

5 Preheat the broiler. Remove the dishes from the refrigerator and sprinkle 1 tablespoon of the raw sugar over each, ensuring that the custard is completely covered.

6 Cook under the preheated broiler for 5–6 minutes or until the sugar has melted and begun to caramelize. Remove from the broiler, let cool slightly, then chill again in the refrigerator for at least 1 hour. Serve immediately.

INGREDIENTS
Serves 6

1½ cups fresh raspberries
½ cup sugar
5 medium egg yolks
2 cups heavy cream
1 tsp. vanilla extract
6 squares white chocolate, chopped
6 tbsp. raw sugar

Helpful Hint

If your broiler does not get hot enough, you could try using a small blowtorch to caramelize the sugar. Keep the flame moving slowly over the sugar until it is melted and bubbling. Let cool as above.

Chocolate Trifle

1 Slice the chocolate jelly roll thickly, and spread each slice with a little strawberry jelly. Place the jelly-roll slices in the bottom of a trifle dish or glass bowl. Sprinkle over the sherry and brandy and let stand for 10 minutes to let the sherry and brandy soak into the jelly roll. Slice half the strawberries and sprinkle evenly over the jelly roll with half the diced mangoes.

2 Break the chocolate into small pieces and place in a small heatproof bowl set over a saucepan of gently simmering water. Heat gently, stirring occasionally, until the chocolate has melted and is smooth and free from lumps.

3 Blend the custard powder, sugar, and milk to a smooth paste in a bowl, then pour into a heavy saucepan. Place over a gentle heat and cook, stirring constantly, until the custard is smooth and thick. Add the melted chocolate and stir until smooth and blended. Remove from the heat and let cool. Stir in the mascarpone cheese.

4 Spoon the custard mixture over the fruit and chill in the refrigerator for 1 hour. Whip the cream until soft peaks form and pile over the top of the set custard. Sprinkle over the toasted slivered almonds and decorate with the remaining whole strawberries and diced mangoes.

INGREDIENTS
Serves 4

1½ chocolate jelly rolls
4 tbsp. strawberry jelly
3 tbsp. medium sherry
3 tbsp. brandy
3 cups fresh strawberries
2 small mangoes, peeled, pitted, and diced
7 squares unsweetened chocolate
2 tbsp. custard powder
2 tbsp. granulated sugar
1¼ cups whole milk
1 cup mascarpone cheese
1 cup heavy cream
3 tbsp. toasted slivered almonds

Tasty Tip

If you prefer, use fresh custard sauce. Heat gently, then stir in the chocolate and mascarpone cheese. Omit the custard powder, sugar, and milk.

Chocolate Profiteroles

1 Preheat the oven to 425° F. Lightly grease 2 baking sheets. For the pastry, place the water and the butter in a heavy saucepan and bring to a boil. Remove from the heat and beat in the flour. Return to the heat and cook for 1 minute or until the mixture forms a ball in the center of the saucepan.

2 Remove from the heat and let cool slightly, then gradually beat in the eggs, a little at a time, beating well after each addition. Once all the eggs have been added, beat until the paste is smooth and glossy. Pipe or spoon 20 small balls onto the baking sheets, allowing plenty of room for expansion.

3 Bake in the preheated oven for 25 minutes or until well risen and golden brown. Reduce the oven temperature to 350°F. Make a hole in each ball and continue to bake for an additional 5 minutes. Remove from the oven and let cool.

4 For the custard sauce, place the milk and nutmeg in a small heavy saucepan, and bring to a boil. In another small heavy saucepan, beat together the egg yolks, sugar, and the flours, then beat in the hot milk. Bring to a boil and simmer, beating constantly for 2 minutes. Cover and let cool.

5 Spoon the custard into the profiteroles and then arrange the profiteroles on a large serving dish. Place all the sauce ingredients in a small, heavy saucepan and bring to a boil, then simmer for 10 minutes. Remove the saucepan from the heat and let cool slightly before serving with the chocolate profiteroles.

INGREDIENTS
Serves 4

FOR THE PASTRY:
⅔ cup water
½ stick butter
⅔ cup all-purpose flour, sifted
2 medium eggs, lightly beaten

FOR THE CUSTARD SAUCE:
1¼ cups milk
pinch of freshly grated nutmeg
3 medium egg yolks
¼ cup sugar
2 tbsp. all-purpose flour, sifted
2 tbsp. cornstarch, sifted

FOR THE SAUCE:
¾ cup firmly packed brown sugar
⅔ cup boiling water
1 tsp. instant coffee
1 tbsp. unsweetened cocoa
1 tbsp. brandy
¾ stick butter
1 tbsp. corn syrup

Chocolate Chip Ice Cream

1 Simmer the raspberries with the sugar and lemon juice for 5 minutes. Let cool, then purée in a food processor. Press through a fine strainer to remove the pips. Set the coulis aside.

2 Pour the milk into a heavy saucepan and add the vanilla pod. Slowly bring to a boil, then remove from the heat and let infuse for 30 minutes. Remove the vanilla pod.

3 Beat the egg yolks and sugar together in a large bowl until pale and creamy, then gradually beat in the infused milk. Strain the mixture into a clean saucepan, place over a gentle heat, and bring slowly to a boil. Cook over a gentle heat, stirring constantly until the mixture thickens and coats the back of a wooden spoon. Do not let the mixture boil, otherwise it will curdle. Once thickened, cover the mixture with a piece of plastic wrap and let the custard cool completely.

4 Break half the chocolate into small pieces and place in a heatproof bowl set over a saucepan of gently simmering water. Heat gently, stirring frequently, until the chocolate has melted and smooth. Remove from the heat and let cool.

5 Whip the cream until soft peaks form and fold into the cooled custard. Coarsely chop the remaining chocolate and stir into the custard mixture, along with the melted chocolate. Spoon into a suitable container and freeze for an hour.

6 Remove from the freezer and beat well to break up all the ice crystals. Repeat the beating and freezing process twice more, then freeze for 4 hours or until the ice cream is solid. Allow to soften in the refrigerator for 30 minutes before serving with fresh fruit and the raspberry coulis. Remember to return the freezer to its normal setting.

INGREDIENTS
Serves 4

3 cups fresh raspberries, or frozen and thawed

¼ cup confectioners' sugar, or to taste

2 tbsp. lemon juice

2½ cups milk

1 vanilla pod, seeds removed

6 medium egg yolks

½ cup sugar

16 squares unsweetened chocolate

½ cup heavy cream

fresh fruit of your choice, to serve

Helpful Hint

If you prefer, you can use a food processor to beat the ice cream as described in step 6.

Rich Chocolate & Orange Mousse

1 Grease and line a loaf pan with plastic wrap, taking care to keep the plastic wrap as wrinkle free as possible. Arrange the sponge ladyfingers around the edge of the loaf pan, trimming to fit if necessary.

2 Place the chocolate, butter, and orange flower water in a heavy saucepan and heat gently, stirring occasionally until the chocolate has melted and is smooth. Remove from the heat, and add the cocoa and ¼ cup of the confectioners' sugar. Stir until smooth, then beat in the egg yolks.

3 In a clean, grease-free bowl, beat the egg whites until stiff but not dry. Sift in the remaining confectioners' sugar, and beat until stiff and glossy. Fold the egg white mixture into the chocolate mixture and, using a metal spoon or rubber spatula, stir until well blended.

4 Spoon the mousse mixture into the prepared loaf pan and level the surface. Cover and chill in the refrigerator until set.

5 Meanwhile, place the sugar with ⅔ cup of water in a heavy saucepan and heat until the sugar has dissolved. Bring to a boil and boil for 5 minutes. Add the orange slices and simmer for about 2–4 minutes or until the slices become opaque. Drain on absorbent paper towels, and set aside.

6 Trim the top of the ladyfingers to the same level as the mousse. Invert onto a large serving plate, and remove the pan and plastic wrap.

7 Whip the cream until soft peaks form, and spoon into a decorating bag fitted with a star-shaped tip. Pipe swirls on top of the mousse and decorate with the orange slices. Chill in the refrigerator before serving.

INGREDIENTS
Serves 8

8–12 sponge ladyfingers
8 squares unsweetened chocolate, broken into pieces
2 sticks unsalted butter
2 tbsp. orange flower water
⅓ cup unsweetened cocoa, sifted
½ cup confectioners' sugar, sifted
5 medium eggs, separated
¼ cup sugar
1 orange, thinly sliced
1 cup heavy cream

Helpful Hint

When filling a decorating bag, try to avoid air pockets, which will making piping quite difficult.

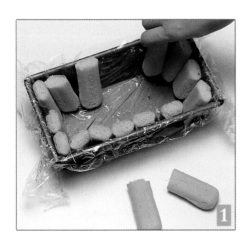

Chocolate & Rum Truffles

1 For the chocolate truffles, break the chocolate into pieces and place in a heatproof bowl set over a saucepan of gently simmering water. Leave for 20 minutes or until the chocolate has melted. Stir until the chocolate is smooth, and remove from the heat. Let stand for about 6 minutes.

2 Beat the butter, egg yolks, brandy or kirsch, and heavy cream together until smooth. Stir the melted chocolate into the butter and egg yolk mixture and stir until thick. Cover and let cool for about 30 minutes. Chill in the refrigerator for 1½ hours or until firm.

3 Divide the truffle mixture into 24 pieces and mold around the drained cherries. Roll in the unsweetened cocoa until evenly coated. Place the truffles in petit-four paper cases and chill in the refrigerator for 2 hours before serving.

4 To make the rum truffles, break the chocolate into small pieces and place in a heavy saucepan with the cream and rum. Heat gently until the chocolate has melted, then stir until smooth. Stir in the ground almonds, pour into a small bowl, and chill in the refrigerator for at least 6 hours or until the mixture is thick.

5 Remove the truffles from the refrigerator and shape small spoonfuls, about the size of a cherry, into balls. Roll in the sifted confectioners' sugar and place in petit-four paper cases. Store the truffles in the refrigerator until ready to serve.

INGREDIENTS
Makes 44

FOR THE CHOCOLATE TRUFFLES:

8 squares unsweetened chocolate

¼ stick butter, softened

2 medium egg yolks

2 tsp. brandy or kirsch

2 tsp. heavy cream

24 maraschino cherries, drained

2 tbsp. unsweetened cocoa, sifted

FOR THE RUM TRUFFLES:

4 squares unsweetened chocolate

2 tbsp. rum

½ cup heavy cream

½ cup ground almonds

2 tbsp. confectioners' sugar, sifted

Tasty Tip

These truffles are so easy to make, they are great to give as gifts. Roll some in confectioners' sugar, as above, and roll others in cocoa. Arrange in a gift box in a checkerboard pattern.

Apricot & Almond Layer Cake

1 Preheat the oven to 350° F. Lightly grease and line 2 9-inch round cake pans. Cream the butter and sugar together until light and fluffy, then beat in the egg yolks, one at a time, beating well after each addition. Stir in the cooled chocolate with 1 tablespoon of cooled boiled water, then fold in the flour and ground almonds.

2 Beat the egg whites until stiff, then gradually beat in the confectioners' sugar, beating well after each addition. Beat until stiff and glossy, then fold the egg whites into the chocolate mixture in 2 batches.

3 Divide the batter evenly among the prepared pans and bake in the preheated oven for 30–40 minutes or until firm.

Leave for 5 minutes before turning out onto wire racks. Let cool completely.

4 Split the cakes in half. Gently heat the jelly, pass through a strainer, and stir in the amaretto liqueur. Place one cake layer onto a serving plate. Spread with a little of the jelly, then sandwich with the next layer. Repeat with all the layers and use any remaining jelly to brush over the entire cake. Leave until the jelly sets.

5 Meanwhile, beat the butter and chocolate together until smooth, then cool at room temperature until thick enough to spread. Cover the top and sides of the cake with the chocolate frosting, and let set before slicing and serving.

INGREDIENTS
Cuts into 8–10 slices

1¼ sticks unsalted butter, softened

½ cup sugar

5 medium eggs, separated

5 squares unsweetened chocolate, melted and cooled

1¼ cups self-rising flour, sifted

½ cup ground almonds

¾ cup confectioners' sugar, sifted

¾ cup apricot jelly

1 tbsp. amaretto liqueur

1 stick unsalted butter, melted

4 squares unsweetened chocolate, melted

Helpful Hint

Use a very good quality apricot jelly, as it is a major flavor in the finished cake.

Black & White Torte

1 Preheat the oven to 350° F. Lightly grease and line a 9-inch round cake pan. Beat the eggs and sugar in a large bowl until thick and creamy. Sift together the cornstarch, all-purpose flour, and self-rising flour 3 times, then lightly fold into the egg mixture.

2 Spoon the batter into the prepared pan and bake in the preheated oven for 35–40 minutes or until firm. Turn the cake out onto a wire rack and let cool.

3 Place 1 cup of the heavy cream in a saucepan and bring to a boil. Immediately remove from the heat, and add the unsweetened chocolate and an additional tablespoon of the liqueur. Stir until smooth. Repeat, using the remaining cream, white chocolate, and liqueur. Chill in the refrigerator for 2 hours, then beat each mixture until thick and creamy.

4 Place the unsweetened chocolate mixture in a decorating bag fitted with a plain tip, and place half the white chocolate mixture in a separate decorating bag fitted with a plain tip. Set aside the remaining white chocolate mixture.

5 Split the cold cake horizontally into two layers. Brush or drizzle the remaining liqueur over the cakes. Put one layer onto a serving plate. Pipe alternating rings of white and dark chocolate mixture to cover the first layer of cake. Use the white chocolate mixture to cover the top and sides of the cake. Dust with unsweetened cocoa, cut into slices, and serve. Store in the refrigerator.

INGREDIENTS
Cuts into 8–10 slices

4 medium eggs
⅔ cup sugar
½ cup cornstarch
½ cup all-purpose flour
½ cup self-rising flour
3 cups heavy cream
5 squares unsweetened chocolate, chopped
11 squares white chocolate, chopped
6 tbsp. Grand Marnier or other orange-flavored liqueur
unsweetened cocoa, for dusting

Mocha Truffle Cake

1 Preheat the oven to 350° F. Lightly grease and line a deep 9-inch round cake pan. Beat the eggs and sugar in a bowl until thick and creamy.

2 Sift together the cornstarch, self-rising flour, and cocoa, and fold into the egg mixture. Spoon into the prepared pan, and bake in the preheated oven for 30 minutes or until firm. Turn out onto a wire rack and leave until cool. Split the cooled cake horizontally into two layers. Mix together the milk and coffee liqueur, and brush onto the cake layers.

3 Stir the cooled white chocolate into one bowl and the cooled unsweetened chocolate into another one. Whip the cream until soft peaks

form, then divide among the two bowls and stir. Place one layer of cake in a 9-inch springform pan. Spread with half the white chocolate cream. Top with the unsweetened chocolate cream, then the remaining white chocolate cream, and finally place the remaining cake layer on top. Chill in the refrigerator for 4 hours or until set.

4 When ready to serve, melt the semisweet chocolate and butter in a heatproof bowl set over a saucepan of simmering water, and stir until smooth. Remove from the heat and leave until thick enough to spread, then use to cover the top and sides of the cake. Allow to set at room temperature, then chill in the refrigerator. Cut the cake into slices and serve.

INGREDIENTS
Cuts into 8–10 slices

3 medium eggs
½ cup sugar
⅓ cup cornstarch
⅓ cup self-rising flour
2 tbsp. unsweetened cocoa
2 tbsp. milk
2 tbsp. coffee liqueur
3½ squares white chocolate, melted and cooled
7 squares unsweetened chocolate, melted and cooled
2 cups heavy cream
7 squares semisweet chocolate
¾ stick unsalted butter

Helpful Hint

Unless you are going to make a lot of chocolate or coffee desserts, liqueurs are very expensive to buy. Look for generic brands or miniatures.

Double Marble Cake

1 Preheat the oven to 350° F. Lightly grease and line the bottom of an 8-inch cake pan. Break the white and unsweetened chocolate into small pieces, then place in 2 separate bowls placed over 2 saucepans of simmering water, ensuring that the bowls are not touching the water. Heat the chocolate until melted.

2 In a large bowl, cream the sugar and butter together until light and fluffy. Beat in the egg yolks, one at a time, and add a spoonful of flour after each addition. Stir in the ground almonds. In another bowl beat the egg whites until stiff. Gently fold in the egg whites and the remaining sifted flour alternately into the almond mixture until all the flour and egg whites have been incorporated. Divide the batter among 2 bowls. Gently stir the white chocolate into one bowl, then add the unsweetened chocolate to the other bowl.

3 Place alternating spoonfuls of the chocolate batters in the prepared cake pan. Using a toothpick, swirl the batters together to get a marbled effect, then tap the pan on the work surface to level the batter. Bake in the preheated oven for 40 minutes or until cooked through. Let cool for 5 minutes in the pan, then turn out onto a wire rack to cool completely.

4 Melt the chocolate with the cream and butter, and stir until smooth. Cool, then beat until thick, and swirl over the top of the cake. Serve.

INGREDIENTS
Cuts into 8–10 slices

3 squares white chocolate
3 squares unsweetened chocolate
¾ cup sugar
1½ sticks butter
4 medium eggs, separated
1 cup all-purpose flour, sifted
¾ cup ground almonds

FOR THE TOPPING:
2 squares white chocolate, chopped
3 squares unsweetened chocolate, chopped
¼ cup heavy cream
¾ stick unsalted butter

Helpful Hint

Place a folded dishtowel under the mixing bowl when creaming or mixing by hand. This keeps the bowl from slipping around.

Chocolate Buttermilk Cake

1 Preheat the oven to 350° F. Lightly grease and line a deep 9-inch round cake pan. Cream together the butter, vanilla extract, and sugar until light and fluffy, then beat in the egg yolks, one at a time.

2 Sift together the flour and cocoa and fold into the egg mixture together with the buttermilk. Beat the egg whites until soft peaks form, and fold carefully into the chocolate mixture in 2 batches. Spoon the batter into the prepared pan, and bake in the preheated oven for 1 hour or until firm. Cool slightly, then turn out onto a wire rack and leave until completely cooled.

3 Place the chocolate and butter together in a heatproof bowl set over a saucepan of simmering water, and heat until melted. Stir until smooth, then leave at room temperature until the chocolate is thick enough to spread.

4 Split the cake horizontally in half. Use some of the chocolate mixture to sandwich the 2 halves together. Spread and decorate the top of the cake with the remaining chocolate mixture. Finally, whip the cream until soft peaks form and use to spread around the sides of the cake. Chill in the refrigerator until required. Serve cut into slices. Store in the refrigerator.

INGREDIENTS
Cuts into 8–10 slices

1½ sticks butter

1 tsp. vanilla extract

1½ cups sugar

4 medium eggs, separated

¾ cup self-rising flour

¼ cup unsweetened cocoa

¼ cup buttermilk

7 squares unsweetened chocolate

¾ stick butter

1 cup heavy cream

Tasty Tip

If buttermilk is unavailable, measure ¼ cup of whole milk and add 2 teaspoons of lemon juice or white wine vinegar. Allow to stand for 1 hour at room temperature and then use as above.

Peach & White Chocolate Cake

1 Preheat the oven to 325° F. Lightly grease and line a deep 9-inch round cake pan. Cream the butter, orange rind, and sugar together until light and fluffy. Add the eggs, one at a time, beating well after each addition, then beat in the cooled white chocolate.

2 Add the flour and ¾ cup of water in two batches. Spoon into the prepared pan and bake in the preheated oven for 1½ hours or until firm. Allow to stand for at least 5 minutes before turning out onto a wire rack to cool completely.

3 To make the filling, place the peaches in a bowl and pour over the liqueur. Allow to stand for 30 minutes. Whip the cream with the confectioners' sugar until soft peaks form, then fold in the peach mixture.

4 Split the cooled cake into three layers, place one layer on a serving plate, and spread with half the peach filling. Top with a second sponge layer and spread with the remaining peach filling. Top with remaining cake.

5 Whip the cream and confectioners' sugar together until soft peaks form. Spread over the top and sides of the cake, piping some onto the top if desired. Press the hazelnuts into the side of the cake and, if desired, sprinkle a few on top. Serve cut into slices. Store in the refrigerator.

INGREDIENTS
Cuts into 8–10 slices

1½ sticks unsalted butter, softened

2 tsp. grated orange rind

¾ cup sugar

3 medium eggs

3½ squares white chocolate, melted and cooled

2 cups self-rising flour, sifted

1 cup heavy cream

⅓ cup confectioners' sugar

1 cup hazelnuts, toasted and chopped

FOR THE PEACH FILLING:

2 ripe peaches, peeled and chopped

2 tbsp. peach or orange liqueur

1 cup heavy cream

⅓ cup confectioners' sugar

Tasty Tip
When fresh peaches are out of season, use drained and chopped canned peaches instead.

Dark Chocolate Layered Torte

1 Preheat the oven to 300° F. Lightly grease and line a 9-inch square cake pan. Melt the butter in a saucepan, remove from the heat, and stir in the coffee granules and 1 cup hot water. Add the unsweetened chocolate and sugar, and stir until smooth, then pour into a bowl.

2 In another bowl, sift together the flours and unsweetened cocoa. Using an electric mixer, beat the sifted mixture into the chocolate mixture until smooth. Beat in the eggs and vanilla extract. Pour into the pan and bake in the preheated oven for 1¼ hours or until firm. Leave for at least 5 minutes before turning out onto a wire rack to cool.

3 Meanwhile, mix together 7 squares of the melted unsweetened chocolate with the butter and confectioners' sugar, and beat until smooth. Let cool, then beat again. Set aside 4–5 tablespoons of the chocolate filling.

4 Cut the cooled cake in half to make 2 rectangles, then split each rectangle in three horizontally. Place one cake layer on a serving plate and spread thinly with the jelly, and then a thin layer of unsweetened chocolate filling. Top with a second cake layer and sprinkle with a little liqueur, then spread thinly with filling. Repeat with remaining cake layers, liqueur, and filling.

5 Chill in the refrigerator for 2–3 hours or until firm. Cover the cake with the chocolate filling and press the slivered almonds into the sides of the cake.

6 Place the remaining melted chocolate in a nonstick baking parchment decorating bag. Snip a small hole in the tip and pipe thin lines, ¾ inch apart, crosswise over the cake. Drag a toothpick lengthwise through the frosting in alternating directions to create a feathered effect. Serve.

INGREDIENTS
Cuts into 10–12 slices

1½ sticks butter

1 tbsp. instant coffee grounds

5 squares unsweetened chocolate

1½ cups sugar

1¼ cups self-rising flour

1 cup all-purpose flour

2 tbsp. unsweetened cocoa

2 medium eggs

1 tsp. vanilla extract

7½ squares unsweetened chocolate, melted

1 stick butter, melted

⅓ cup confectioners' sugar, sifted

2 tsp. raspberry jelly

2½ tbsp. chocolate liqueur

¾ cup toasted slivered almonds

Tasty Tip

For the best flavor, use unsweetened chocolate that has 70 percent cocoa solids.

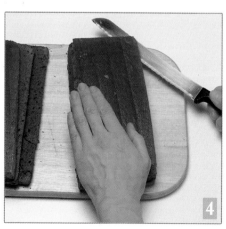

Chocolate Mousse Sponge

1 Preheat the oven to 350° F. Lightly grease and line a 9-inch round cake pan, and lightly grease the sides of a 9-inch springform pan. Beat the eggs, sugar, and vanilla extract until thick and creamy. Fold in the flour, ground almonds, and unsweetened chocolate. Spoon the batter into the prepared round cake pan and bake in the preheated oven for 25 minutes or until firm. Turn out onto a wire rack to cool.

2 For the mousse, soak the gelatin in ¼ cup of cold water for 5 minutes until softened. Meanwhile, heat the heavy cream in a small saucepan. When almost boiling, remove from the heat and stir in the chocolate and vanilla extract. Stir until the chocolate melts. Squeeze the excess water out of the gelatin and add to the chocolate mixture. Stir until dissolved, then pour into a large bowl.

3 Beat the egg whites until stiff, then gradually add the sugar, beating well between each addition. Fold the egg white mixture into the chocolate mixture in two batches.

4 Split the cake into 2 layers. Place one layer in the bottom of the springform pan. Pour in the chocolate mousse mixture, then top with the second layer of cake. Chill in the refrigerator for 4 hours or until the mousse has set. Loosen the sides and remove the cake from the pan. Dust with confectioners' sugar and decorate the top with a few freshly sliced strawberries. Serve cut into slices.

INGREDIENTS
Cuts into 8–10 slices

3 medium eggs
⅓ cup sugar
1 tsp. vanilla extract
½ cup self-rising flour, sifted
¼ cup ground almonds
2 squares unsweetened chocolate, grated
confectioners' sugar, for dusting
freshly sliced strawberries, to decorate

FOR THE MOUSSE:
2 sheets gelatin
¼ cup heavy cream
3½ squares unsweetened chocolate, chopped
1 tsp. vanilla extract
4 medium egg whites
½ cup sugar

Tasty Tip

Sheet gelatin is very easy to use. Soak the gelatin as described in step 2, then squeeze out the excess liquid. It must be added to hot liquid, where it will melt on contact.

Chocolate Chiffon Cake

1 Preheat the oven to 325° F. Lightly grease and line a 9-inch round cake pan. Lightly grease a baking sheet. Blend the unsweetened cocoa with ¾ cup of boiling water, and let cool. Place the flour and 1½ cups of the sugar in a large bowl, and add the cocoa mixture, egg yolks, oil, and vanilla extract. Beat until smooth and lighter in color.

2 Beat the egg whites in a clean, grease-free bowl until soft peaks form, then fold into the cocoa mixture.

3 Pour into the prepared pan and bake in the preheated oven for 1 hour or until firm. Leave for 5 minutes before turning out onto a wire rack to cool.

4 To make the frosting, cream together 1 stick of the butter with the confectioners' sugar, unsweetened cocoa, and brandy until smooth, then set aside. Melt the remaining butter and blend with 5 squares of the melted unsweetened chocolate. Stir until smooth and then leave until thickened.

5 Place the remaining sugar into a small, heavy saucepan over a low heat and heat until the sugar has melted and is a deep golden brown.

6 Add the walnuts and the remaining melted chocolate to the melted sugar and pour onto the prepared baking sheet. Leave until cold and brittle, then chop finely. Set aside.

7 Split the cake into 3 layers, place one layer onto a large serving plate, and spread with half of the brandy butter frosting. Top with a second cake layer, spread with the remaining brandy butter frosting, and arrange the third cake layer on top. Cover the cake with the thickened chocolate glaze. Sprinkle with the walnut praline and serve.

INGREDIENTS
Cuts into 10–12 slices

½ cup unsweetened cocoa
2¾ cups self-rising flour
2½ cups sugar
7 medium eggs, separated
¼ cup vegetable oil
1 tsp. vanilla extract
¾ cup walnuts
2 squares unsweetened chocolate
7 squares unsweetened chocolate, melted

FOR THE FROSTING:
1½ sticks butter
2½ cups confectioners' sugar, sifted
2 tbsp. unsweetened cocoa, sifted
2 tbsp. brandy

Helpful Hint

Do not overmix the mixture in step 2 or the cake will be heavy instead of light and spongy.

White Chocolate & Passion Fruit Cake

1 Preheat the oven to 350° F. Lightly grease and line 2 8-inch cake pans.

2 Melt the white chocolate in a heatproof bowl set over a saucepan of simmering water. Stir in ½ cup warm water and stir, then let cool.

3 Beat the butter and sugar together until light and fluffy, and add the eggs, one at a time, beating well after each addition. Beat in the chocolate mixture, sour cream, and sifted flours. Divide the batter into 8 portions. Spread one portion into each of the pans. Bake in the preheated oven for 10 minutes or until firm, then turn out onto wire racks. Repeat with the remaining mixture to make 8 cake layers.

4 To make the frosting, place ½ cup of water with ¼ cup of the sugar in a saucepan. Heat gently, stirring, until the sugar has dissolved. Bring to a boil, and simmer for 2 minutes. Remove from the heat and cool, then add 2 tablespoons of the passion fruit juice. Set aside.

5 Blend the remaining sugar with ¼ cup of water in a small saucepan, and stir constantly over a low heat, without boiling, until the sugar has dissolved. Remove from the heat and cool. Stir in the remaining passion fruit juice and the seeds. Cool, then strain. Using an electric mixer, beat the butter in a bowl until very pale. Gradually beat in the syrup.

6 Place one layer of cake on a large serving plate. Brush with the syrup and spread with a thin layer of frosting. Repeat with the remaining cake, syrup, and frosting. Cover the cake with the remaining frosting. Press the chocolate curls into the top and sides to decorate.

INGREDIENTS
Cuts into 8–10 slices

4 squares white chocolate
1 stick butter
1 cup sugar
2 medium eggs
½ cup sour cream
1¾ cups all-purpose flour, sifted
¾ cup self-rising flour, sifted
4 squares white chocolate, coarsely grated, to decorate

FOR THE FROSTING:

1 cup sugar
4 tbsp. passion fruit juice (about 8–10 passion fruit, strained)
1½ tbsp. passion fruit seeds
2¼ sticks unsalted butter

Food Fact

Passion fruit is increasingly available from large supermarkets. It adds a sweet and sour flavor that goes well with white chocolate.

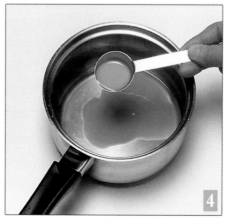

Sachertorte

1 Preheat the oven to 350° F. Lightly grease and line a deep 9-inch cake pan.

2 Melt the 5 squares of chocolate in a heatproof bowl set over a saucepan of simmering water. Stir in 1 tablespoon of water and allow to cool.

3 Beat the butter and ½ cup of the sugar together until light and fluffy. Beat in the egg yolks, one at a time, beating well between each addition. Stir in the melted chocolate, then the flour.

4 In a clean, grease-free bowl, beat the egg whites until stiff peaks form, then beat in the remaining sugar. Fold into the chocolate mixture and spoon into the prepared pan. Bake in the preheated oven for 30 minutes or until firm. Leave for 5 minutes, then turn out onto a wire rack to cool. Leave the cake upside down.

5 To decorate the cake, split the cold cake in two and place one half on a serving plate. Heat the jelly and rub through a fine strainer.

6 Brush half the jelly onto the first cake half, then cover with the remaining cake layer and brush with the remaining jelly. Leave for 1 hour or until the jelly has set.

7 Place the unsweetened chocolate and the butter into a heatproof bowl set over a saucepan of simmering water, and heat until the chocolate has melted. Stir occasionally until smooth, then leave until thickened. Use to cover the cake.

8 Melt the semisweet chocolate in a heatproof bowl set over a saucepan of simmering water. Place in a small waxed decorating bag and snip a small hole at the tip. Pipe "Sacher" with a large "S" on the top. Allow to set at room temperature.

INGREDIENTS
Cuts into 10–12 slices

5 squares unsweetened chocolate
1¼ sticks unsalted butter, softened
½ cup sugar, plus 2 tbsp.
3 medium eggs, separated
1¼ cups all-purpose flour, sifted

TO DECORATE:
⅔ cup apricot jelly
4 squares unsweetened chocolate, chopped
1 stick unsalted butter
1 square semisweet chocolate

Food Fact

In 1832, the Viennese foreign minister asked a Vienna hotel to prepare an especially tempting cake. The head pastry chef was ill and so the task fell to second-year apprentice, Franz Sacher, who presented this delightful cake.

Chocolate Roulade

1 Preheat the oven to 350° F. Lightly grease and line a 9 inch x 13 inch jelly-roll pan with nonstick baking parchment.

2 Break the chocolate into small pieces into a heatproof bowl set over a saucepan of simmering water. Leave until almost melted, stirring occasionally. Remove from the heat and let stand for 5 minutes.

3 Beat the egg yolks with the sugar until pale and creamy and the whisk leaves a trail in the mixture when lifted. Carefully fold in the melted chocolate.

4 In a clean, grease-free bowl, beat the egg whites until stiff, then fold one large spoonful into the chocolate mixture.

5 Mix lightly, then gently fold in the remaining egg whites. Pour the batter into the prepared pan and level the surface. Bake in the preheated oven for 20–25 minutes or until firm.

6 Remove the cake from the oven, leave in the pan, and cover with a wire rack and a damp dishtowel. Leave for 8 hours or preferably overnight.

7 Dust a large sheet of nonstick baking parchment generously with 2 tablespoons of the confectioners' sugar. Unwrap the cake and turn out onto the waxed paper. Remove the baking parchment.

8 Whip the cream with the liqueur until soft peaks form. Spread over the cake, leaving a 1-inch border all around.

9 Using the paper to help, roll the cake up from a short end. Transfer to a serving plate, seam-side down, and dust with the remaining confectioners' sugar. Decorate with fresh raspberries and mint. Serve.

INGREDIENTS
Cuts into 8 slices

7 squares unsweetened chocolate

1 cup sugar

7 medium eggs, separated

1 cup heavy cream

3 tbsp. Cointreau or Grand Marnier

4 tbsp. confectioners' sugar, for dusting

TO DECORATE:
fresh raspberries
sprigs of fresh mint

Tasty Tip

Leaving the cake in the pan overnight gives it a fudgy texture and also means that the cake is less likely to break when it is rolled up.

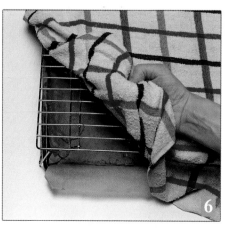

Supreme Chocolate Cake

1 Preheat the oven to 350° F. Lightly grease and line 3 8-inch round cake pans. Place all the cake ingredients into a bowl and beat together until thick. Add a little warm water if too thick. Divide the batter evenly among the prepared pans. Bake in the preheated oven for 35–40 minutes until a toothpick inserted in the center comes out clean. Cool on wire racks.

2 Very gently, heat 2 tablespoons of hot water with 2 squares of chocolate, and stir until combined. Remove from the heat and leave for 5 minutes. Place the gelatin into a shallow dish and add 2 tablespoons of cold water. Leave for 5 minutes, then squeeze out any excess water and add to the chocolate and water mixture. Stir until dissolved. Whip the heavy cream until just thickened. Add the chocolate mixture and continue beating until soft peaks form. Leave until starting to set.

3 Place one of the cakes onto a serving plate and spread with half the cream mixture. Top with a second cake and the remaining cream, cover with the third cake, and chill in the refrigerator until set.

4 Melt 6 squares of the chocolate with the butter, and stir until smooth. Allow to thicken. Melt the remaining chocolate. Cut 12 4-inch squares of foil. Spread the chocolate evenly over the squares to within 1 inch of the edges. Refrigerate for 3–4 minutes until just set but not brittle. Gather up the corners and crimp together. Return to the refrigerator until firm.

5 Spread the chocolate and butter mixture over the top and sides of the cake. Remove the foil from the giant curls and use to decorate the top of the cake. Dust with unsweetened cocoa and serve cut into wedges.

INGREDIENTS
Cuts into 10–12 slices

FOR THE CAKE:
1½ cups self-rising flour, sifted
1½ tsp. baking powder, sifted
3 tbsp. unsweetened cocoa, sifted
1½ sticks butter, softened
¾ cup sugar
3 large eggs

TO DECORATE:
12 squares unsweetened chocolate
1 gelatin leaf
1 cup heavy cream
¾ stick butter
unsweetened cocoa, for dusting

Helpful Hint

If you prefer, make ordinary chocolate curls to decorate this cake.

Chocolate Hazelnut Meringue Cake

1 Preheat the oven to 300° F. Cut 3 pieces of nonstick baking parchment into 12 5-inch rectangles, and then place onto 2 or 3 baking sheets.

2 Beat the egg whites until stiff, add half the sugar, and beat until the mixture is stiff, smooth, and glossy. Beat in the remaining sugar, 1 tablespoon at a time, beating well between each addition. When all the sugar has been added, beat for 1 minute. Stir in the hazelnuts.

3 Spoon the meringue inside the marked rectangles, spreading in a continuous backward and forward motion. Bake in the preheated oven for 1¼ hours, remove, and leave until cold. Trim the meringues until they measure 4 x 10 inches. Set aside all the trimmings.

4 Melt the chocolate and the butter in a heatproof bowl set over a saucepan of gently simmering water and stir until smooth. Remove from the heat and beat in the egg yolks. Beat the egg whites until stiff, then beat in the confectioners' sugar, a little at a time. Fold the egg whites into the chocolate mixture and chill in the refrigerator for 20–30 minutes until thick enough to spread. Whip the heavy cream until soft peaks form. Set aside.

5 Place one of the meringue layers onto a serving plate. Spread with about half of the mousse mixture, then top with a second meringue layer. Spread the remaining mousse mixture over the top with the third meringue. Spread the cream over the top and sprinkle with the hazelnuts. Chill in the refrigerator for at least 4 hours. Serve.

INGREDIENTS
Cuts into 8–10 slices

5 medium egg whites

1¼ cups sugar

1 cup hazelnuts, toasted and finely chopped

6 squares unsweetened chocolate

¾ stick butter

3 medium eggs, separated, plus 1 medium egg white

¼ cup confectioners' sugar

½ cup heavy cream

hazelnuts, toasted and chopped, to decorate

Tasty Tip

This cake can be round. Make the meringues into circles measuring 8 inches. Trim to 7 inches before assembling.

Black Forest Cake

1 Preheat the oven to 300° F. Lightly grease and line a deep 9-inch cake pan.

2 Melt the butter in a large saucepan. Blend the coffee with the hot water, add to the butter with the chocolate and sugar, and heat gently, stirring until smooth. Pour into a large bowl and leave until just warm.

3 Sift together the flours and unsweetened cocoa. Using an electric mixer, beat the warm chocolate mixture on a low speed, then gradually beat in the dry ingredients. Beat in the eggs one at a time, then add the vanilla extract.

4 Pour the batter into the prepared pan and bake in the preheated oven for 1 hour and 45 minutes or until firm and a toothpick inserted into the center comes out clean. Leave the cake in the pan for 5 minutes to cool slightly before turning out onto a wire rack.

5 Place the cherries and their juice in a small saucepan and heat gently.

6 Blend the arrowroot with 2 teaspoons of water until smooth, then stir into the cherries. Cook, stirring until the liquid thickens. Simmer very gently for 2 minutes, then leave until cooled.

7 Beat the heavy cream until thick. Trim the top of the cake if necessary, then split the cake into 3 layers.

8 Brush the bottom of the cake with half the kirsch. Top with a layer of cream and one-third of the cherries. Repeat the layering, then place the third layer on top.

9 Set aside a little cream for decorating and use the remainder to cover the top and sides of the cake. Pipe a decorative edge around the cake, then arrange the remaining cherries in the center and serve.

INGREDIENTS
Cuts 10–12 slices

2¼ sticks butter

1 tbsp. instant coffee grounds

1½ cups hot water

7 squares unsweetened chocolate, chopped or broken

1¾ cups sugar

2 cups self-rising flour

1¼ cups all-purpose flour

½ cup unsweetened cocoa

2 medium eggs

2 tsp. vanilla extract

2 14-oz. cans pitted cherries in juice

2 tsp. arrowroot

2 cups heavy cream

¼ cup kirsch

Helpful Hint

The cake can be assembled and served right away but will benefit from being refrigerated for 1–2 hours so that the cream sets slightly. This will make slicing easier.

Whole Orange & Chocolate Cake with Marmalade Cream

1 Preheat the oven to 350° F. Lightly grease and line the bottom of a loaf pan. Place the orange in a small saucepan, cover with cold water, and bring to a boil. Simmer for 1 hour or until completely soft. Drain and let cool.

2 Place 2 egg yolks, 1 whole egg, and the sugar in a heatproof bowl set over a saucepan of simmering water, and beat until doubled in bulk. Remove from the heat and continue to beat for 5 minutes until cooled.

3 Cut the whole orange in half and discard the seeds, then place into a food processor or blender and blend to a purée.

4 Carefully fold the purée into the egg yolk mixture with the ground almonds and melted chocolate.

5 Beat the egg whites until stiff peaks form. Fold a large spoonful of the egg whites into the chocolate mixture, then gently fold the remaining egg whites into the mixture.

6 Pour into the prepared pan and bake in the preheated oven for 50 minutes or until firm and a toothpick inserted into the center comes out clean. Cool in the pan before turning out of the pan and carefully discarding the lining paper.

7 Meanwhile, whip the heavy cream until just thickened. In another bowl, blend the cream cheese with the confectioners' sugar and marmalade until smooth, then fold in the heavy cream.

8 Chill the marmalade cream in the refrigerator until needed. Decorate with orange zest, cut in slices, and serve with the marmalade cream.

INGREDIENTS
Cuts 6–8 slices

1 small orange, scrubbed

2 medium eggs, separated, plus 1 whole egg

1¼ cups sugar

1 cup ground almonds

3 squares unsweetened chocolate, melted

½ cup heavy cream

¾ cup cream cheese

¼ cup confectioners' sugar

2 tbsp. orange marmalade

orange zest, to decorate

Tasty Tip

This cake contains no flour and is therefore likely to sink in the center on cooling. This is normal and does not mean that the cake is not cooked.

Grated Chocolate Roulade

1 Preheat the oven to 350° F. Lightly grease and line an 8 x 12 inch jelly-roll pan. Beat the egg yolks and sugar with an electric mixer for 5 minutes or until thick, then stir in 2 tablespoons of hot water and the grated chocolate. Fold in the sifted flour.

2 Beat the egg whites until stiff, then fold 1–2 tablespoons of egg white into the chocolate mixture. Mix lightly, then gently fold in the remaining egg white. Pour into the prepared pan and bake in the preheated oven for about 12 minutes or until firm.

3 Place a large sheet of nonstick baking parchment onto a work surface and sprinkle liberally with sugar. Turn the cake onto the baking parchment, discard the lining paper, and trim away the crisp edges. Roll up as for a jelly-roll cake, leave for 2 minutes, then unroll and let cool.

4 Beat the heavy cream with the confectioners' sugar and vanilla extract until thick. Set aside a little for decoration, then spread the remaining cream over the cake, leaving a 1-inch border all around. Using the waxed paper, roll up from a short end.

5 Carefully transfer the roulade to a large serving plate, and use the cream to decorate the top. Add the chocolate curls just before serving, then cut into slices and serve. Store in the refrigerator

INGREDIENTS
Cuts 8 slices

4 medium eggs, separated
½ cup sugar
2½ squares unsweetened chocolate, grated
¾ cup self-rising flour, sifted
2 tbsp. sugar, plus extra for sprinkling
½ cup heavy cream
2 tsp. confectioners' sugar
1 tsp. vanilla extract
chocolate curls, to decorate

Helpful Hint

Make sure to leave a border around the cream before rolling up the roulade, or all the cream will squeeze out of the ends.

White Chocolate & Raspberry Mousse Cake

1 Preheat the oven to 375° F. Grease and line 2 9-inch cake pans. Beat the eggs and sugar until thick and creamy and the whisk leaves a trail in the mixture. Fold in the flour and cornstarch, then divide among the pans. Bake in the preheated oven for 12–15 minutes or until risen and firm. Cool in the pans, then turn out onto wire racks.

2 Place the gelatin with 4 tablespoons of cold water in a dish and let soften for 5 minutes. Purée half the raspberries, press through a strainer, then heat until nearly boiling. Squeeze out excess water from the gelatin, add to the purée, and stir until dissolved. Set aside.

3 Melt 6 squares of the chocolate in a bowl set over a saucepan of simmering water. Let cool, then stir in the yogurt and purée. Beat the egg whites until stiff and beat in the sugar. Fold into the raspberry mixture with the rest of the raspberries.

4 Line the sides of a 9-inch springform pan with nonstick baking parchment. Place one layer of sponge in the bottom and sprinkle with half the liqueur. Pour in the raspberry mixture and top with the second sponge. Brush with the remaining liqueur. Press down and chill in the refrigerator for 4 hours. Unmold onto a plate.

5 Cut a strip of double-thick nonstick baking parchment to fit around the cake and stand ½ inch higher. Melt the remaining white chocolate and spread thickly onto the paper. Leave until just setting. Wrap around the cake and freeze for 15 minutes. Peel away the paper. Whip the cream until thick and spread over the top. Decorate with raspberries.

INGREDIENTS
Cuts 8 slices

4 medium eggs
½ cup sugar
¾ cup all-purpose flour, sifted
¼ cup cornstarch, sifted
3 gelatin leaves
4 cups raspberries, thawed if frozen
14 squares white chocolate
¾ cup plain yogurt
2 medium egg whites
2 tbsp. sugar
4 tbsp. raspberry or orange liqueur
¾ cup heavy cream
fresh raspberries, halved, to decorate

Helpful Hint

Don't try to wrap the chocolate-covered parchment around the cake before it's set, or it will run and be uneven.

Chocolate Orange Fudge Cake

1 Preheat the oven to 350° F. Lightly grease and line 2 9-inch round cake pans with nonstick baking parchment. Blend the unsweetened cocoa and ¼ cup of boiling water until smooth. Stir in the orange zest and set aside. Sift together the flour, baking powder, baking soda, and salt, then set aside. Cream together the sugar and softened butter, and beat in the eggs, one at a time, then the cocoa mixture and vanilla extract. Finally, stir in the flour mixture and the sour cream in alternating spoonfuls.

2 Divide the batter among the prepared pans and bake in the preheated oven for 35 minutes or until the edges of the cake pull away from the pan and the tops spring back when lightly pressed. Cool in the pans for 10 minutes, then turn out onto wire racks until cold.

3 Gently heat the butter and milk with the pared orange rind. Simmer for 10 minutes, stirring occasionally. Remove from the heat and discard the orange rind.

4 Pour the warm orange and milk mixture into a large bowl and stir in the unsweetened cocoa. Gradually beat in the sifted confectioners' sugar and beat until the frosting is smooth and spreadable. Place one cake onto a large serving plate. Top with about one-quarter of the frosting, place the second cake on top, then cover the cake with the remaining frosting. Serve.

INGREDIENTS
Cuts into 8–10 slices

⅔ cup unsweetened cocoa

1 tbsp. grated orange zest

3 cups self-rising flour

2 tsp. baking powder

1 tsp. baking soda

½ tsp. salt

1 cup firmly packed golden brown sugar

1½ sticks butter, softened

3 medium eggs

1 tsp. vanilla extract

1⅛ cup sour cream

6 tbsp. butter

6 tbsp. milk

thinly pared rind of 1 orange

6 tbsp. unsweetened cocoa

2¼ cups confectioners' sugar, sifted

Helpful Hint

This cake keeps exceptionally well in an airtight container for up to five days.

Cranberry & White Chocolate Cake

1 Preheat the oven to 350° F. Lightly grease and flour a 9-inch fancy tube mold (kugelhopf pan) or ring mold. Using an electric mixer, cream the butter and cheese with the sugars until light and fluffy. Add the grated orange zest and vanilla extract, and beat until smooth. Beat in the eggs, one at a time.

2 Sift the flour and baking powder together, and stir into the creamed batter, beating well after each addition. Fold in the cranberries and 6 squares of the white chocolate. Spoon into the prepared mold and bake in the preheated oven for 1 hour or until firm and a toothpick inserted into the center comes out clean. Cool in the mold before turning out onto on a wire rack.

3 Melt the remaining white chocolate, stir until smooth, then stir in the orange juice and let cool until thickened. Transfer the cake to a serving plate and spoon over the white chocolate and orange glaze. Allow to set.

INGREDIENTS
Serves 4

2 sticks butter, softened

1⅛ cup cream cheese

⅔ cup firmly packed golden brown sugar

1 cup sugar

3 tsp. grated orange zest

1 tsp. vanilla extract

4 medium eggs

3¼ cups all-purpose flour

2 tsp. baking powder

¾ cup cranberries, thawed if frozen

8 squares white chocolate, coarsely chopped

2 tbsp. orange juice

Tasty Tip

If fresh or frozen cranberries are not available, substitute chopped dried apples, raisins, dried cranberries, or chopped dried apricots.

Helpful Hint

A kugelhopf pan is a ring mold with fluted sides that makes a decoratively shaped cake. A kugelhopf is a German cake made with yeast, and is similar to a panettone.

INDEX